presents

Crafts In Minutes

presents

Crafts In Minutes

Oxmoor House®

Crafts In Minutes

Book Division of Southern Progress Corporation
P.O. Box 2463, Birmingham, Alabama 35201

Published by Oxmoor House, Inc., and Leisure Arts, Inc.

Library of Congress Catalog Card Number: 97-65076
Hardcover ISBN: 0-8487-1649-3
Softcover ISBN: 0-8487-1651-5
Manufactured in the United States of America
First Printing 1997

Lifetime Entertainment Services, Inc.
Alan Gabay
Cecelia K. Toth

Oxmoor House, Inc.
Editor-in-Chief: Nancy Fitzpatrick Wyatt
Senior Homes Editor: Mary Kay Culpepper
Senior Editor, Editorial Services: Olivia Kindig Wells
Art Director: James Boone

Crafts In Minutes
Editors: Susan Hernandez Ray, Adrienne E. Short
Associate Art Director: Cynthia R. Cooper
Designer: Clare T. Minges
Editorial Assistant: Cecile Y. Nierodzinski
Copy Editor: L. Amanda Owens
Illustrator: Kelly Davis
Senior Photographer: John O'Hagan
Photo Stylist: Connie Formby
Production and Distribution Director: Phillip Lee
Associate Production Managers: Theresa L. Beste, Vanessa Cobbs Richardson

We're here for you!
We at Oxmoor House are dedicated to serving you with reliable information that expands your imagination and enriches your life. We welcome your comments and suggestions. Please write us at:

Oxmoor House, Inc.
Editor, *Crafts In Minutes*
2100 Lakeshore Drive
Birmingham, AL 35209

To order additional publications, call 1-205-877-6560.

Contents

Great Gifts

Giving a great gift is as easy as picking your favorite project. Indulge luxury-loving friends with botanical bath oils bottled in recycled glass. Give all your packages extra flair with mailing-tag gift cards embellished with stamps created from foam trays. Make a baby shower extra special with decorated rompers made with iron-on transfers or pretty paper frames mixed in the blender.

page 10

page 8

page 12

page 16

Put Your Stamp on It

Cut a grocery store foam tray into stylish stamps to decorate great gifts.

Gift Tags

Lampshade

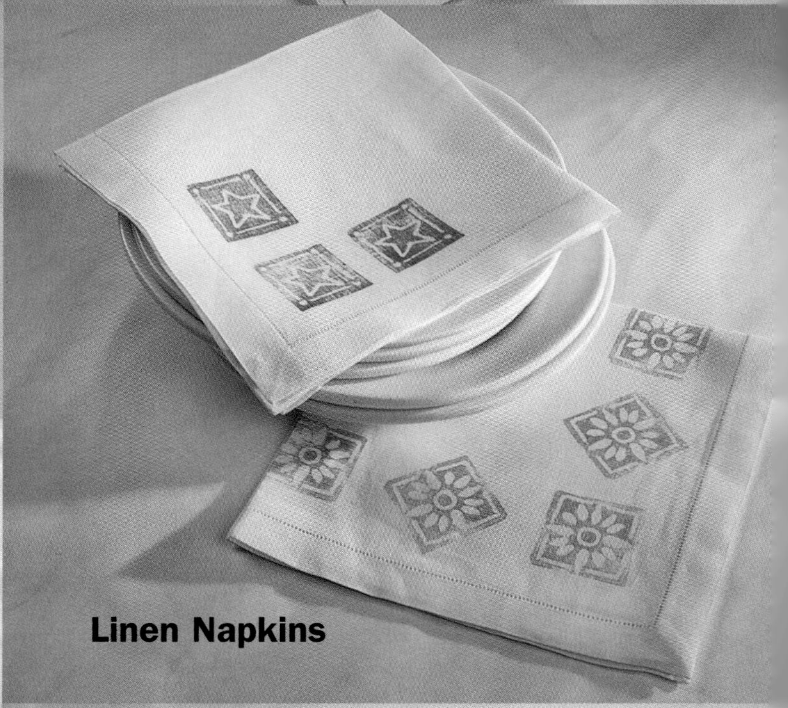

Linen Napkins

Trinket Box

Photo Mats

You will need:

tracing paper
clean, dry grocery store foam tray
ballpoint pen
masking tape
object to be stamped (We used manila mailing tags, 5" lampshade, linen napkins, painted wooden box, and mat board.)
pigment ink: navy, magenta, periwinkle
artist's fixative or acrylic spray varnish

1. For stamp, trace desired pattern onto tracing paper. Cut 2" square from foam tray. Center pattern on top of foam square. Using tip of ballpoint pen, trace pattern, applying enough pressure to make imprint in foam. Remove pattern and retrace design to make deeper imprint in foam. Do not let pen point break through stamp.

2. To create large negative space in design, such as flower petals and center of sun, press down inside each selected section to flatten foam.

3. For stamping handle, cut 4" length of masking tape. Fold in half, leaving ends free. Press ends against back of stamp (see photo at right).

4. Practice stamping on scrap paper before stamping actual project. Stamped image will be reverse of pattern. Pattern lines will be thicker on actual project than they appear on stamp. Stamp can be reused with same color ink; make new stamp for each new color.

5. Press stamp against ink pad. Position stamp on object and stamp designs as desired. For **gift tags** with multiple images, lay several mailing tags side by side on protected work surface. Stamp design in diagonal rows across all tags (see photo at right). For **lampshade**, to stamp onto curved surface, place 1 edge of stamp on shade and slowly roll to opposite edge of stamp. Repeat on shade as many times as desired. For **napkins**, center first stamped design 2" from 1 corner of napkin. Continue stamping until desired effect is achieved. For **trinket box**, center design on box lid. For **photo mat**, cut mat board to desired size. (We used 5" x 7" mat with 3"-square opening for photo.) Stamp as desired.

6. For fabric or paper projects, spray finished item with fixative. For remaining projects, spray item with varnish. Let dry overnight.

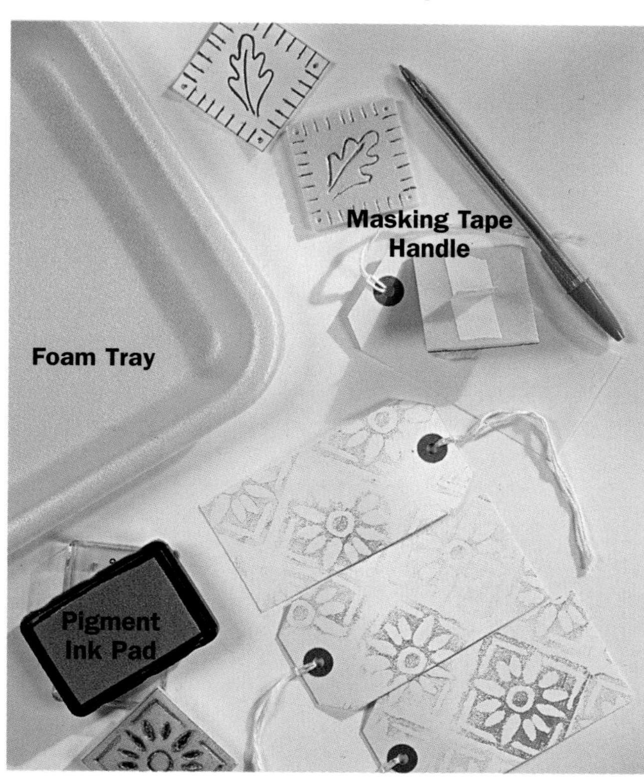

Foam trays are soft enough to mark with a ballpoint pen yet substantial enough to stamp over and over again. To make a stamp, simply trace the pattern onto a square of foam to make an imprint. For ease, add a masking tape handle.

FLOWER

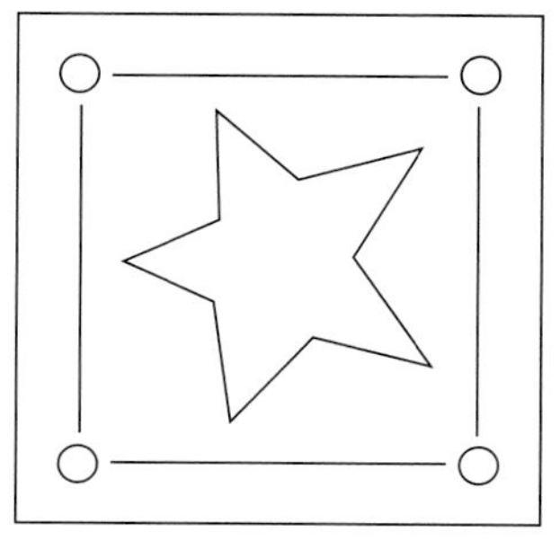

STAR

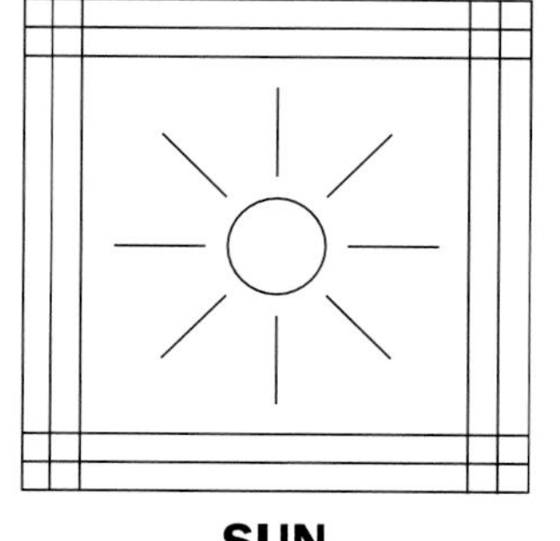

SUN

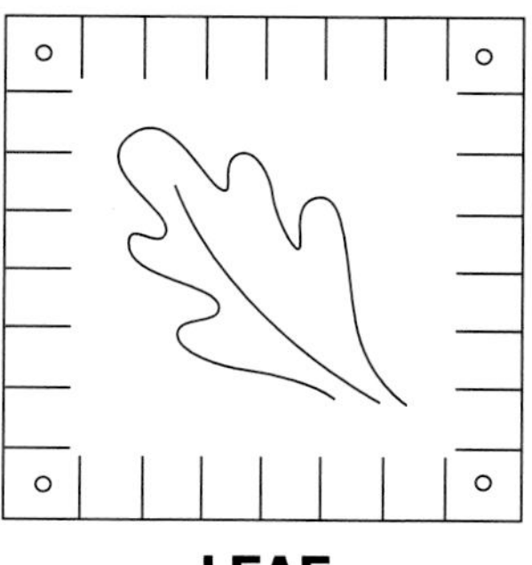

LEAF

Fragrant Bath Oils

Compared to store-bought versions, these luxurious homemade oils are money-saving presents.

Chamomile Oil

Lavender Oil

The recipes that follow use common ingredients often sold at the grocery store or pharmacy.

You will need (for each):

clean, dry bottle with cork stopper (We used 16- to 24-ounce bottle.)
funnel

For Chamomile Oil:
pesticide-free dried yarrow, safflower, or strawflower
avocado oil (to fill bottle)
chamomile essential oil (for fragrance)

For Lavender Oil:
pesticide-free dried lavender and/or rosemary
mineral oil (to fill bottle)
lavender essential oil (for fragrance)

For Vanilla-Almond Oil:
pesticide-free globe amaranth, rosebuds, and/or Russian statice
1 part mineral oil and 1 part almond oil (to fill bottle)
vanilla essential oil (for fragrance)

For Rosebud Oil:
pesticide-free dried lavender, rosebuds, or globe amaranth
mineral oil (to fill bottle)
rose essential oil (for fragrance)

1. Place desired number of herb and flower sprigs inside bottle, trimming stems as necessary to fit.

2. Using funnel, fill bottle with designated oil.

3. For fragrance, add 4 or 5 drops of essential oil to bottle. (You may add more or less, depending on size of bottle.) Insert cork stopper. Invert bottle gently a few times to blend essential oil. See **Bottle Topper** to decorate bottle for gift-giving.

Bottle Topper

You will need:

paraffin
wax crayons in desired colors
old paintbrush
medium-weight decorative paper
hole punch
raffia

1. Melt paraffin over low heat. Add crayons, 1 at a time, to warm paraffin until desired richness of color is achieved.

2. Using paintbrush, apply paraffin around cork and lip of bottle to seal. Let dry slightly. Invert bottle and dip cork and lip into paraffin several times, letting each coat dry between applications. (Paraffin dries quickly.)

3. For tag to label bottle, cut paper into desired shape. Write name of oil on tag. Punch hole in tag. Tie to bottle with raffia (see photos).

Vanilla-Almond Oil
Rosebud Oil

Handmade Paper Frames

These colorful gifts begin in a blender, so they're easy to whip up.

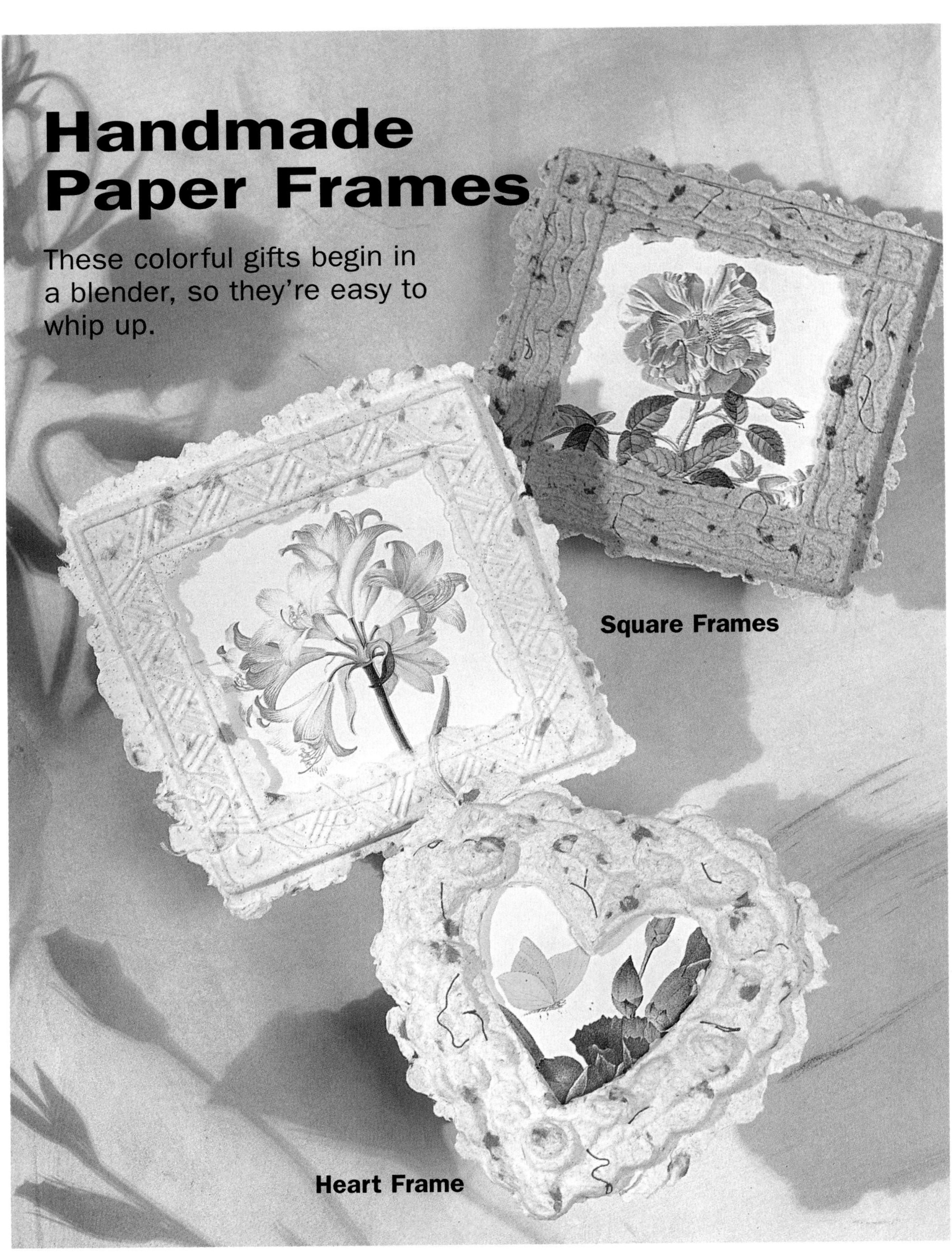

Square Frames

Heart Frame

We used clay cookie molds with interesting border motifs for our square frames.

You will need (for each):

- 1 (7" x 8") sheet 100%-cotton linter paper
- 1 (8½" x 11") sheet construction paper in desired color
- electric blender
- 1 quart cold water
- sieve
- desired clay, plastic, or metal mold
- 2 kitchen dish towels
- embroidery floss
- sponge
- desired print or photo
- craft glue
- 2 sheets mat board or heavy cardboard (cut to same size as mold)

Note: Size of mold will vary amount of pulp needed. Molds shown here are approximate 4" squares and 4" heart.

1. To make paper pulp, tear linter paper into 1" pieces. Beginning with half a sheet, tear construction paper into 1" pieces. (Add more construction paper for darker color.) Place all pieces into blender with cold water. Let soak for 10 minutes **(Photo 1).**

2. Blend for 1 minute at low speed. Check for desired color of pulp. Add more construction paper if needed to achieve desired color. Blend again at high speed for 1 minute.

3. Pour wet pulp into sieve and press to drain as much water as possible. Place mold on 1 folded dish towel. Cut embroidery floss into small pieces and separate into strands. Place as desired inside mold, allowing some floss ends to extend beyond mold **(Photo 2).** Pick up small handfuls of damp pulp and press even layer into border of mold, covering all edges **(Photo 3).**

4. Press pulp into frame with damp sponge; wring out sponge and repeat. Using remaining dish towel, press pulp firmly into mold. Repeat several times to absorb as much water as possible. This ensures that paper will pick up all mold details and prevents a wrinkled finish.

5. To dry pulp in mold, leave on counter overnight, place in oven at 150° for 2 hours, or set outside in sunshine for 4 hours. To dry quickly, use microwave oven: Place mold in center of microwave and cook on HIGH for 1 minute and 30 seconds, rotating mold after 1 minute. Continue microwaving at 30-second intervals until paper is completely dry. Size of mold and climate will vary drying times.

6. When dry, lift edges with thin knife and peel paper carefully out of mold. Scrub mold with brush and hot soapy water to clean.

7. To make frame, center and glue desired print or photo on mat board. Center and glue mat board on back of paper frame. To make stand for square frame from remaining mat board, beginning at 1 bottom corner, cut diagonally up to center. Bend corner out to make stand. For heart frame, cut diagonally up to center from both bottom corners and bend both corners out to make stand. Center and glue stand to back of frame.

Photo 1

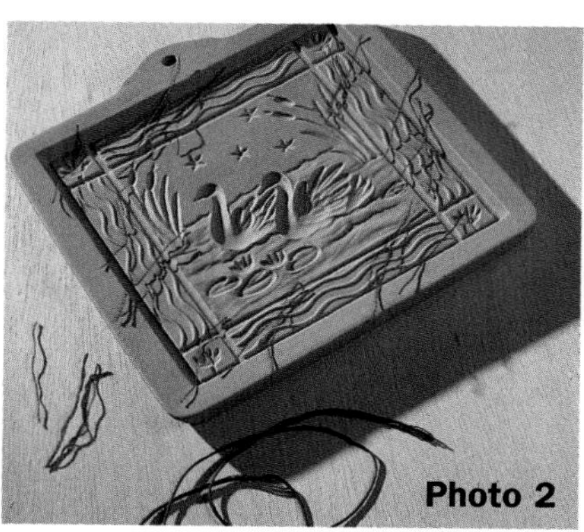
Photo 2

Photo 3

Vintage Wreath

Recycled wine bottle corks encircle this tasteful wreath. Collected bottle labels decorate the bow.

When you remove wine bottle labels, torn edges are fine. They add to this wreath's charm.

You will need:

16"-diameter straw wreath
hot-glue gun with glue sticks
Spanish moss
wine and champagne bottle corks (We used approximately 200 corks to cover this wreath.)
twisted paper roll
craft wire
wine labels
razor blade
craft glue
gold Rub 'n Buff paint
straight pins

1. Using hot glue, cover wreath with Spanish moss. Let dry. Referring to photo, hot-glue corks to front and sides of wreath.

2. For bow, untwist twisted paper and flatten. To make bow, form 1 end of paper into small loop. Loop remaining paper under small loop and make larger loop. Repeat to make 3 more large loops **(Diagram 1).**

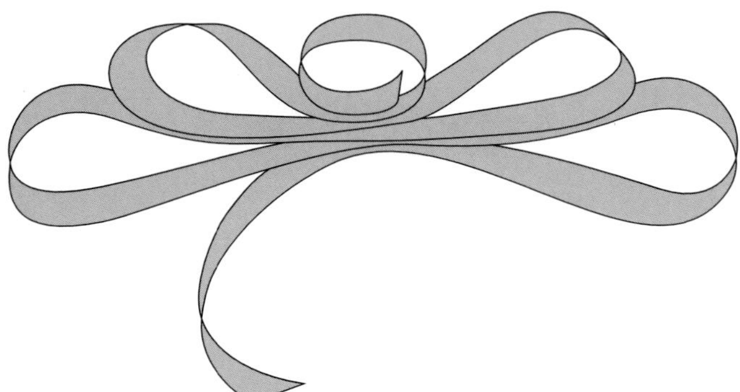

Diagram 1

Cut end of paper after making fourth large loop. Secure loops with craft wire **(Diagram 2).** Cut 1 (1-yard) length of twisted paper. Position bow in center of ribbon length and twist wire to secure.

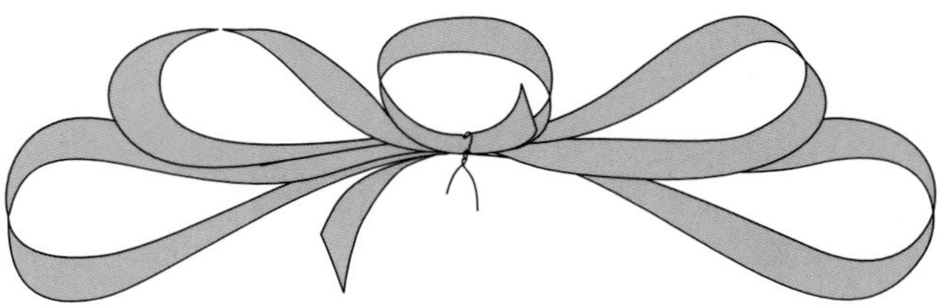

Diagram 2

3. To remove labels, soak wine bottles in warm water for approximately 8 hours or overnight. Remove bottles from water and pat dry. Carefully peel labels from bottles with razor blade, removing as much of each label in 1 piece as possible. (If a label is extremely difficult to remove, continue to soak bottle until you can easily peel back corner of label.) Set labels aside and let dry.

4. Using craft glue, attach labels to bow as desired (see photo). Let dry. With fingertips, lightly rub gold paint over bow and edges of labels. Let dry. Referring to photo, attach bow to wreath with pins, pushing pins into corks.

- For a wreath of "celebration corks," have guests at a party sign and date the corks with a permanent marker.
- Ask your favorite restaurant owner or waiter to save empty wine bottles and corks for you.

Adorable All-in-Ones

Personalize a popular baby shower present with iron-on transfers.

You will need (for each):

baby romper
iron-on transfers (See page 147.)
scrap of fabric or thick paper
straight pins
freezer paper
acrylic paints: yellow, green, orange, red, white, black, brown, blue
textile medium
soft bristle paintbrush
black permanent fabric marker

1. Before transferring design, wash, dry, and iron romper. Do not use fabric softener in washer or dryer. Cut out desired transfer from page 147, leaving as much excess paper around design as possible. Place scrap of fabric or paper inside romper to prevent transfer from bleeding through.

2. Place transfer facedown on right side of romper where desired. Pin in place. Place hot, dry iron on transfer. Do not use steam. Hold iron down for 5 to 10 seconds. Do not slide iron because this might smear design. Continue until all of design is transferred.

3. Turn romper inside out. Reposition scrap of fabric or paper inside romper. Cut freezer paper into 4" x 10" rectangle. Iron freezer paper (waxed side down) onto romper, making sure not to pull design out of shape. (Freezer paper stabilizes the knit fabric for painting.) Turn romper right side out.

4. For each color, mix equal parts paint with textile medium. Referring to photo, paint design with paintbrush. Let paint dry between colors and coats. (We used 2 coats on most areas of each design.) Using fabric marker, outline design details. Heat-set paint with iron. Launder romper according to paint manufacturer's instructions.

For a pretty presentation, stack the folded rompers and tie them together with ribbon. To make a matching gift tag, iron or trace a design onto heavy paper and shade it with colored pencils.

Magnetic Bulletin Boards

A fabric-covered cookie sheet attracts handcrafted plaster magnets.

Blue Gingham Bulletin Board

You will need (for each):

metal cookie sheet
desired fabric
sponge brush
Royal Coat Decoupage Glue
desired trim (We used lace trim for Blue Gingham Bulletin Board.)
Faster Plaster
Faster Plaster Molds: Fruits (#67109), Teapots (#367208)
Faster Plaster Paints
Faster Plaster Matte Glaze
paintbrush
round magnets
hot-glue gun and glue sticks

Green Check Bulletin Board

1. For **bulletin board,** wash cookie sheet with soap and water. Dry thoroughly. Cut fabric to fit front of cookie sheet, including handles (see photos).

2. Using sponge brush, cover front of cookie sheet with decoupage glue. Place fabric over glue. Smooth out wrinkles in fabric with your fingers, pressing from center of cookie sheet out to edges. Using sponge brush, apply coat of decoupage glue over fabric. Let dry. If desired, add lace or ribbon trim around edge of cookie sheet, using decoupage glue. Let dry.

3. For **plaster magnets,** following manufacturer's instructions, mix needed amount of plaster. Pour plaster into desired mold.

4. To quick-dry plaster in microwave, let plaster set in mold for approximately 1 hour. After plaster has set, gently remove pieces from mold. Place pieces on paper towel in microwave oven. Cook on HIGH for 30-second intervals until dry. When dry, remove pieces from microwave and let cool. To air-dry, let plaster set in mold for approximately 6 hours. (Climate and size of mold will vary drying time.)

5. Using paintbrush, paint pieces with colors to coordinate with fabric (see photos). Let dry. Paint pieces with glaze. Let dry. Hot-glue magnets to backs of plaster pieces. Let dry.

tip

To display, prop the board against a wall. If the cookie sheet has a hole in the handle, slip a ribbon through the hole to hang the board.

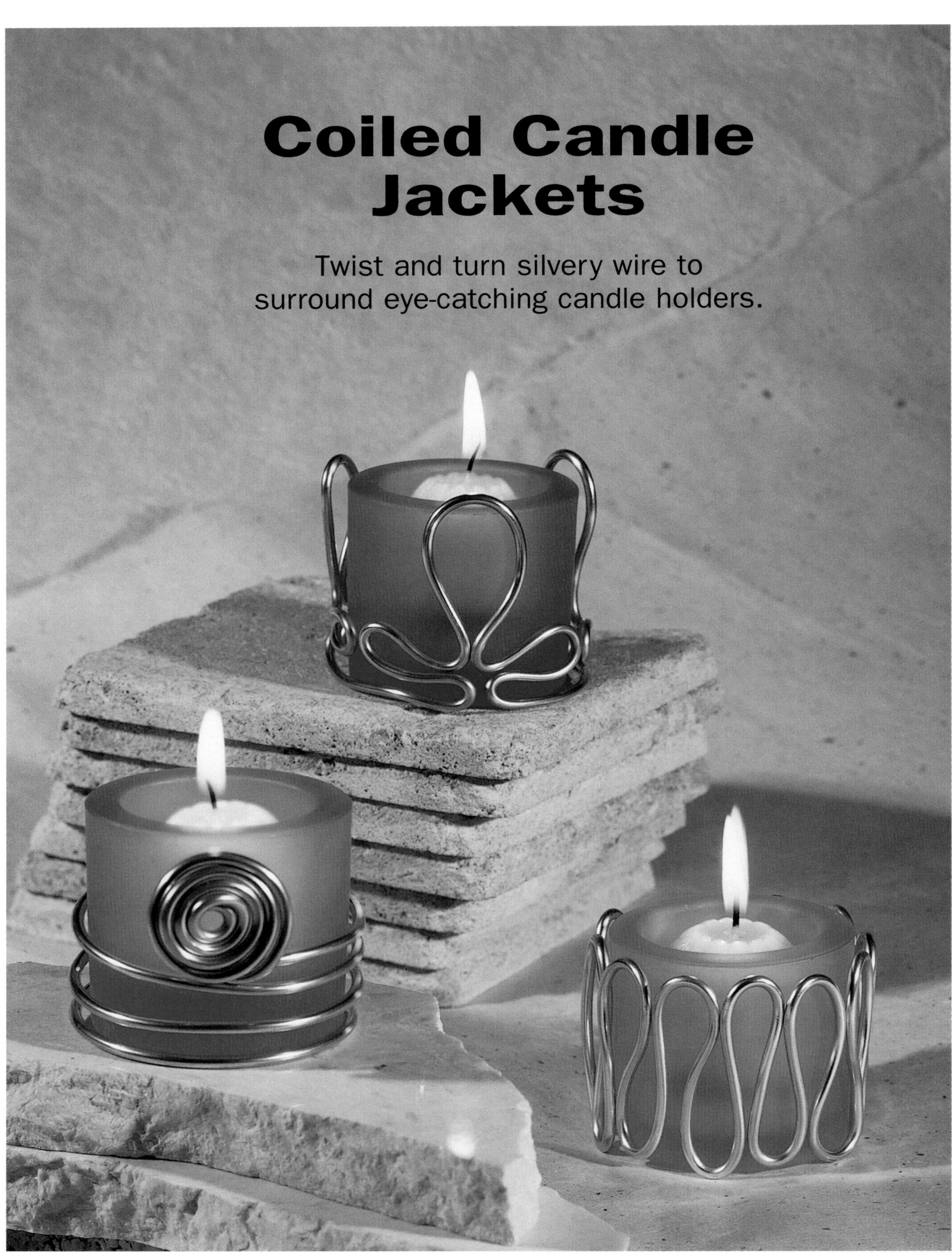

Coiled Candle Jackets

Twist and turn silvery wire to surround eye-catching candle holders.

This tin wire, often called solder, is soft and pliable. To straighten it, slowly and firmly pull the ends like taffy.

You will need (for each):

purchased glass votive candle holder
paper
tape
.125"-diameter silver bearing solder wire
6" length 28-gauge galvanized steel wire
wire cutters
needlenose pliers
gloves (optional)

1. To prevent surface of candle holder from getting scratched while you shape wire, wrap candle holder with piece of paper; tape in place.

2. Measure circumference of candle holder. For desired design, work with wire as it comes off spool. Work wire into flat design to fit around candle holder. Then bend wire design to fit around holder. Clip wire off spool, using wire cutters.

3. For **spiral design,** referring to spiral pattern, form wire into tight curl 2" from wire end, using needlenose pliers. Wrap wire around curl 4 or 5 times with your fingers, increasing size of spiral and keeping spiral flat. If spiral will not stay flat, press spiral facedown on tabletop while wrapping wire around curl. (Protect tabletop with paper.) Hold spiral at top edge of candle holder (see photo at left). Wrap wire around candle holder 4 or 5 times in downward spiral to bottom of holder.

4. For **leaf design,** referring to leaf pattern, form wire into 1 small loop, using needlenose pliers. Then form 1 large loop extending to rim of candle holder and 1 small loop. Repeat until design is length to fit around candle holder.

5. For **ribbon candy design,** referring to ribbon candy pattern, shape curves around your fingers. Extend curves to rim and to bottom of candle holder. Repeat until design is length to fit around candle holder.

6. To secure candle jacket around candle holder, place ends of solder together and tightly wrap 4 or 5 times with 28-gauge wire, using needlenose pliers (see photo below). Twist ends of 28-gauge wire together and bend down ends. Remove protective paper from candle holder and slip finished candle jacket around holder.

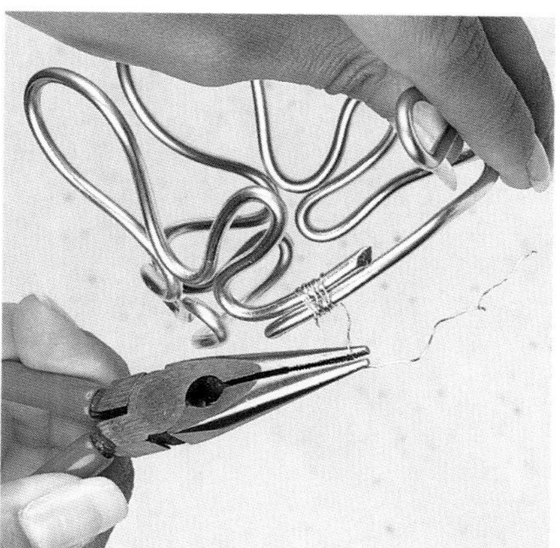
To finish the candle jacket, wrap 28-gauge wire around the ends of the solder 4 or 5 times, using needlenose pliers.

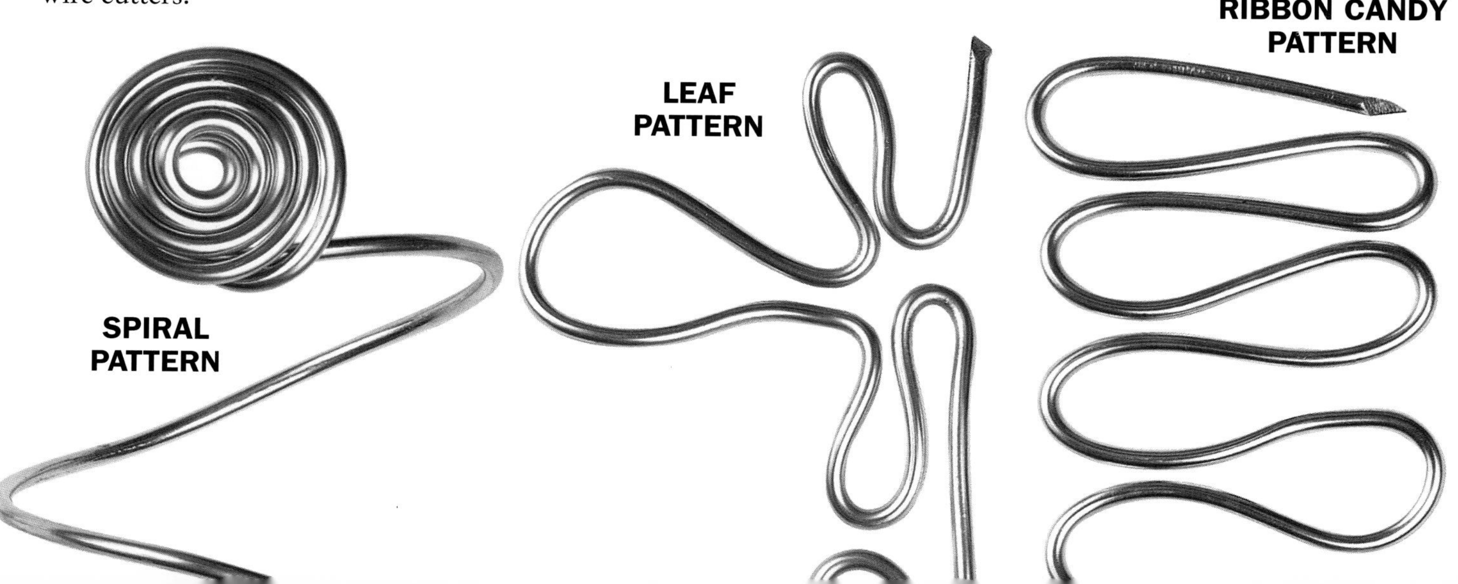

Victorian Preserved Bouquet

Wax-covered flowers, fruits, and vegetables make a beautiful, old-fashioned surprise.

The paraffin coating on the blooms gives them a porcelain-look finish and virtually makes the arrangement last forever.

You will need:

1 (1-pound) box paraffin for 10 items
1 (3-pound) empty coffee can
medium-sized saucepan
fresh, chilled roses
dried hydrangea stems, orange slices, pomegranates, and artichokes
tongs
aluminum foil
wire coat hanger
clothespins
toothpicks
desired container for bouquet arrangement
sheet moss
florist's foam

1. For double boiler, fill saucepan with several inches of water. Place paraffin in coffee can. Set can in saucepan; melt paraffin over low heat.

2. Working with 1 item at a time, carefully dip flower, fruit, or vegetable headfirst into melted paraffin, turning gently until completely coated. To dip flower, hold by stem, using tongs. (To fit inside can, you may have to break large hydrangea blooms into smaller sections.)

3. To dry, remove each paraffin-coated hydrangea stem, orange slice, pomegranate, and artichoke to aluminum foil. To dry each rose, hang upside down from wire hanger, using clothespins to hold stem onto hanger. If necessary, use toothpick to separate flower petals that have stuck together. Let dry. After paraffin dries, cut away excess paraffin around edges of flower, fruit, or vegetable.

4. For arrangement, cover bottom and sides of container with pieces of sheet moss (see photos). Place florist's foam inside container. Referring to photos, arrange paraffin-coated flowers, fruits, and vegetables inside container, pushing stems of flowers into florist's foam to secure.

Waxing works with both fresh and dried flowers, fruits, and vegetables. However, it's best to use fresh, chilled roses so that the wax will capture the pretty shape of the open blooms. And dried hydrangea stalks are preferred because the petals can withstand the hot wax used in the process.

Handmade Journal

This blank book is destined to hold memories and more.

For a rustic style, cover the journal in leather instead of felt and bind an interesting twig to the spine.

You will need:

16" square felt in desired color
masking tape
craft knife
10 (5" x 6⅞") blank greeting cards
hole punch
½ yard 2-mm black leather lacing
black pencil
black dimensional paint

Note: Finished size of journal is approximately 6" x 7½".

1. Measure and cut 7½" x 11¾" piece from felt. To find center, fold piece in half widthwise, aligning edges. Round off corners (see photos). Gently finger-press fold for center. Unfold felt and mark center crease with strip of tape, aligning 1 edge of tape with crease.

2. On each half of felt, ¾" from center, measure and mark 1 hole 2" from top and and 1 hole 2" from bottom, using pencil (see photos). Using craft knife, cut small slit at each mark for lacing. Remove tape.

3. For each card, ½" from folded edge, measure and mark 1 hole 1½" from top and 1 hole 1½" from bottom, using pencil (see photos). Using hole punch, punch holes through front and back of card at each mark for lacing.

4. Cut 2 (8") lengths from lacing. Working from back of right-hand felt half, insert 1 end of 1 lacing piece through 1 hole in felt. Pull lacing halfway through hole to inside of cover. Repeat with remaining lacing piece and remaining hole.

5. To lace each card, insert inside end of lacing pieces through holes in card, positioning card on right-hand half of felt (see photo below). When all cards are laced, align folded edges.

6. Insert inside ends of lacing pieces through holes to outside of left-hand half of felt. Close left-hand felt half over cards and align edges of felt. Referring to photo on front of card, tie ends of each lacing piece together in knot along fold of journal.

7. Slip pencil underneath lacing on top of journal (see photo at left). Using dimensional paint, write desired initials or label on journal cover. Let dry.

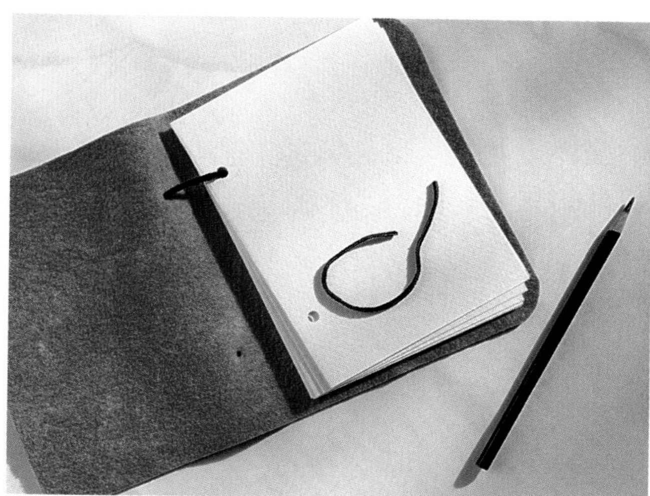

Lace the blank greeting cards inside a piece of thick felt. Leave the folds of the cards uncut to help hold the journal together.

Plate Clock

Give the gift of time by turning a purchased plate into a kitchen clock.

You will need:

10" dinner plate
wire coat hanger
needlenose pliers
gold spray paint
ruler
clear silicone sealer
soft clean cloth
clock works for ¼" thick face

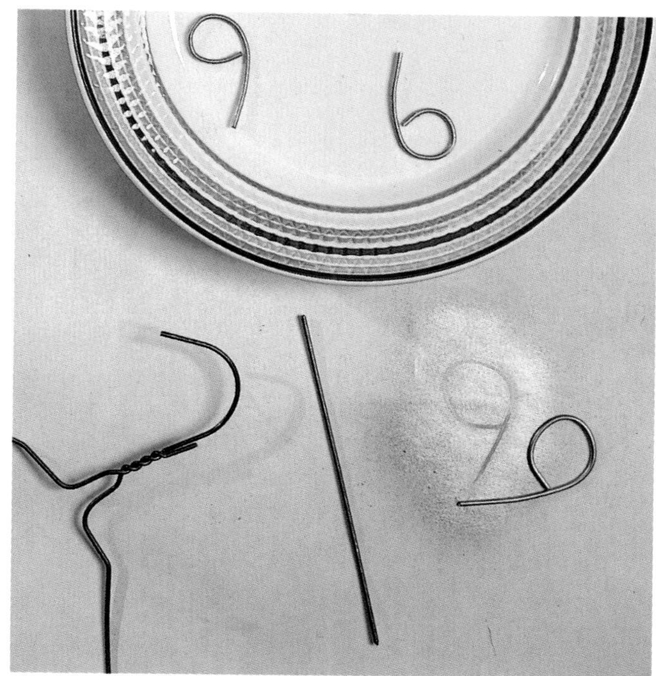

Create numbers by simply cutting and shaping pieces of coat hanger. Finish with a coat of gold spray paint.

Note: Take the plate to a tile or glass company to have a hole drilled in the middle of the plate. Or you can drill the hole yourself with a high speed drill. Place a few drops of water on the desired area and use a ¼" carbide drill bit.

1. Using needlenose pliers, cut and shape coat hanger into desired numbers. Spray with gold paint. Let dry.

2. Determine placement of numbers with ruler. Lightly dab clear silicone sealer on back of numbers and press firmly into place, wiping excess carefully with cloth. Let dry according to manufacturer's directions.

3. Assemble clockworks according to package directions, adhering clock mechanism to plate with silicone sealer.

tip

You can substitute pieces of stained glass, jewelry findings, or 1" tile pieces for numbers.

Fashion Finds

With today's fabrics and materials, you'll find it easy to make fashion to fit your lifestyle. Embellish a cardigan with pearl buttons to make a sporty sweater. For a project that's as much fun to make as it is to wear, mold craft clay into fashionable pendants. Plain cotton T-shirts take on a great new look when their dressed with pearls. Add flair to your wardrobe with scarves you can make with less than a yard of fabric.

page 40
page 46
page 36
page 32

Trimmed Espadrilles

Plain summer shoes go zingy with zigzag stripes.

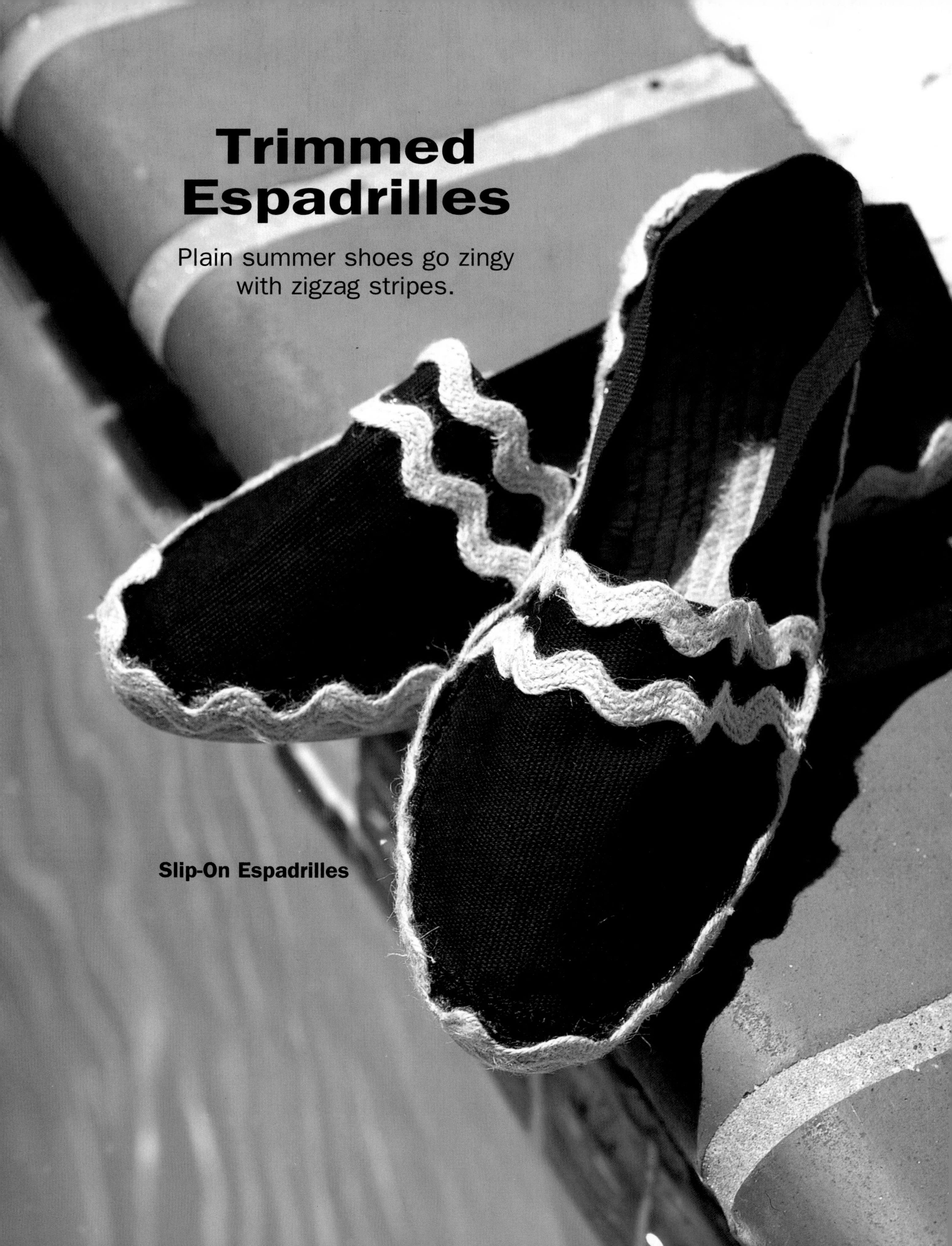

Slip-On Espadrilles

Slip-On Espadrilles

You will need:

1 pair purchased black espadrilles
jute large rickrack: 4 (6½") lengths, 2 (23") lengths
liquid ravel preventer
flexible fabric glue

1. For each shoe, apply liquid ravel preventer to cut ends of rickrack. Center and glue 1 (6½") length of rickrack across top straight edge of shoe (see photo at left). Do not turn raw ends under. Repeat to glue another rickrack length across top of shoe, 1" from first length. Let dry.

2. Beginning at heel, glue 1 (23") length of rickrack around lower edge of shoe, covering raw ends of previously glued rickrack lengths (see photo at left). Trim any excess. Apply liquid ravel preventer to cut end. Let dry.

For added flair, stitch lengths of twill tape to the heel of the shoes to make colorful ankle ties.

Ankle-Tie Espadrilles

You will need:

1 pair purchased white espadrilles
dressmaker's colored pencil
2 (10") lengths each large rickrack: green, blue
flexible fabric glue
green mini rickrack: 4 (10") lengths, 2 (36") lengths
2 (36") lengths blue twill tape
sewing machine (optional)
green thread
liquid ravel preventer

1. For each shoe, referring to photo below, use pencil to lightly mark 4 evenly spaced diagonal lines across top. Start marking at upper inside edge and angle down to outside edge.

2. Fold cut end of 1 length of green large rickrack under ¼". Glue along second line from toe. Trim other end ¼" beyond edge of shoe. Fold cut end under ¼" and glue in place. Repeat to cover third line from toe, using 1 length of blue large rickrack. Let dry.

3. Repeat Step 2 to cover remaining lines on shoe, using 2 (10") lengths of mini rickrack.

4. For ankle tie, referring to photo, center and topstitch 1 (36") mini rickrack length on right side of 1 twill tape length. If using a sewing machine, select multizigzag or wide zigzag stitch to keep mini rickrack flat. Apply liquid ravel preventer to cut ends of twill tape.

5. Fold rickrack-trimmed twill tape in half to mark center; unfold. With wrong side of stitched twill tape facing shoe, tack marked center of twill tape to outside top edge of heel. Tie cut ends of twill tape into knots.

Pearl-Studded T-shirts

Mother always said never leave home without your pearls. And now you won't have to.

Pearl Swirl T-shirt

Pearl Swirl T-shirt

You will need:

plain cotton T-shirt in desired color
cardboard shirt form or large scrap of cardboard
dressmaker's pen
$1\frac{2}{3}$ yards 4-mm pearls-by-the-yard
flexible fabric glue
waxed paper
large book or heavy object for weight

1. Fold shirt in half to find center front of neckline; crease. Insert cardboard into shirt. Pin front of shirt to cardboard to prevent shirt from slipping.

2. Using dressmaker's pen, measure and mark $2\frac{1}{2}$" down from neckline at center. (Center of each swirl will be placed $2\frac{1}{2}$" down from neckline.) Measure and mark 3" from each shoulder seam. Center remaining marks between existing marks (see photo at left).

3. From pearls-by-the yard, cut 5 (12") lengths. On waxed paper, make glue spot a little larger than size of quarter. Place 1 end of 1 pearl length in center of glue spot. Wind pearls to form a tight spiral, adding more glue as needed around edge. Hold in place for a minute while glue begins to set. Then place second piece of waxed paper over swirl and cover with heavy book. Let dry for at least 1 hour. Repeat to make total of 5 swirls.

4. Carefully remove swirls from waxed paper and glue onto marks on shirt. Let dry. Follow glue manufacturer's instructions before wearing and washing shirt.

Pearl Necklace T-shirt

You will need:

plain cotton T-shirt in desired color
cardboard shirt form or large scrap of cardboard
pearls-by-the-yard (See Step 2 for yardage you need.)
flexible fabric glue

1. Insert cardboard into shirt. Pin front of shirt to cardboard to prevent shirt from slipping.

2. To determine yardage of pearls, measure from shoulder seam to shoulder seam, 1" from curve of neckline. Repeat to measure 2 more rows, each $\frac{1}{4}$" apart. Add 3 measurements together to get total yardage of pearls needed. (You may want to buy extra pearls-by-the-yard. It's always easier to cut off extra length than to add more pearls.)

3. Cut pearls into 3 lengths as determined in Step 2. At 1 shoulder seam, 1" from neckline, begin gluing shortest length to shirt. Put small line of glue on shirt at a time. Then press pearls into glue for a few seconds. Continue gluing and pressing pearls around curve of neckline. Repeat for remaining rows of pearls, keeping rows $\frac{1}{4}$" apart.

4. Let dry. Follow glue manufacturer's instructions before wearing and washing shirt.

Pearl Necklace T-shirt

Ribbon Rosette Pin

Bring a blouse into bloom any season of the year.

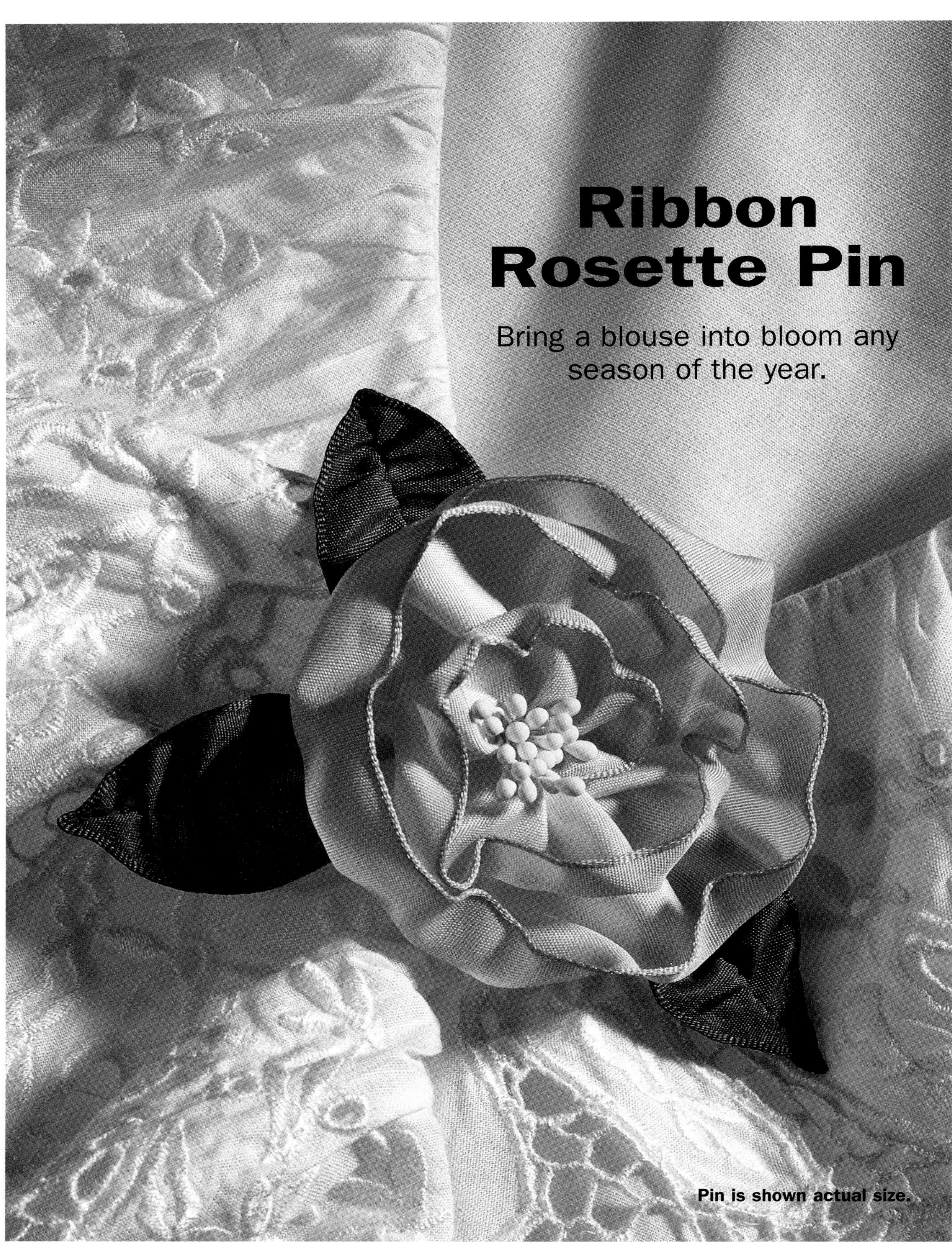

Pin is shown actual size.

You will need:

20" length 1½"-wide wire-edged ribbon, shaded pink to white
tweezers
needle and thread to match ribbons
10 light yellow craft flower stamens
12" length 1½"-wide wire-edged ribbon, shaded green to peach
straight pins
1½"-long pin back

Note: Finished size of pin is approximately 4" in diameter.

1. To gather pink ribbon into rosette, fold in half, matching cut ends. Trim ends at angle so that white edge is shorter than pink edge. To gather 1 half of ribbon, using tweezers, gently pull wire along white edge **(Diagram 1).** (Wire is soft and can break.) Gather until you reach ribbon center. Knot wire to secure. Repeat to gather other half of ribbon.

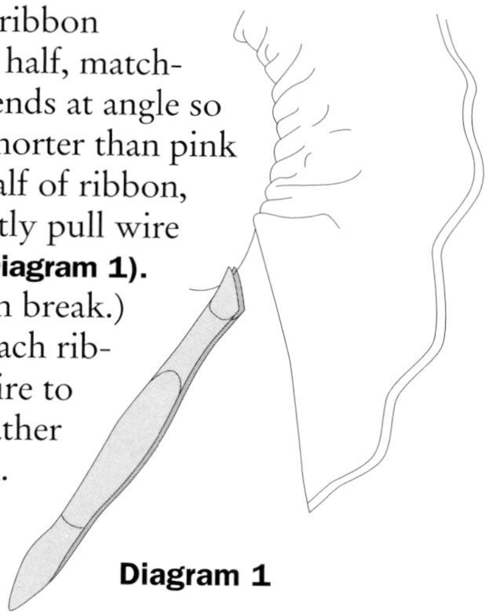

Diagram 1

2. Using needle and thread, run small gathering stitches ¼" from each cut end of ribbon. Pull threads to gather and knot to secure.

3. For flower center, fold stamens in half. Coil 1 short gathered end of ribbon around stamens. Handstitch ribbon to stamens. Coil long gathered edge of ribbon around stamens, stitching at ¼" intervals to secure. Stitch end of ribbon to center to conceal raw edges **(Diagram 2).**

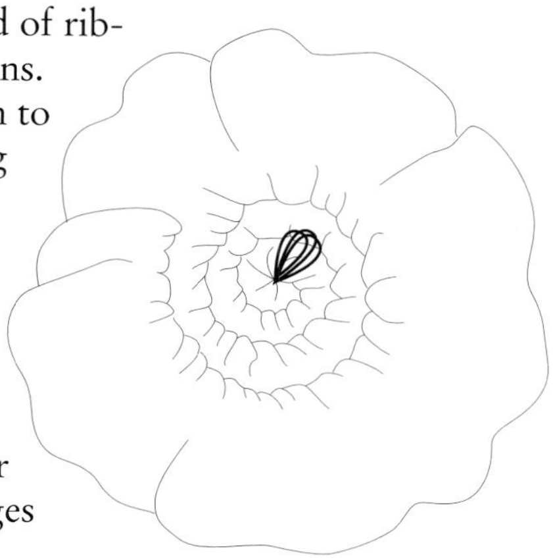

Diagram 2

4. For each leaf, cut 1 (5½") length from green ribbon. With wrong sides together, fold ribbon in half, matching cut ends; pin. Place 1 long wire edge of ribbon on straight edge of leaf pattern **(Diagram 3).** Align folded end of ribbon with pattern where indicated. Mark curved edge of pattern. Handstitch along marked line. Trim ⅛" from stitching.

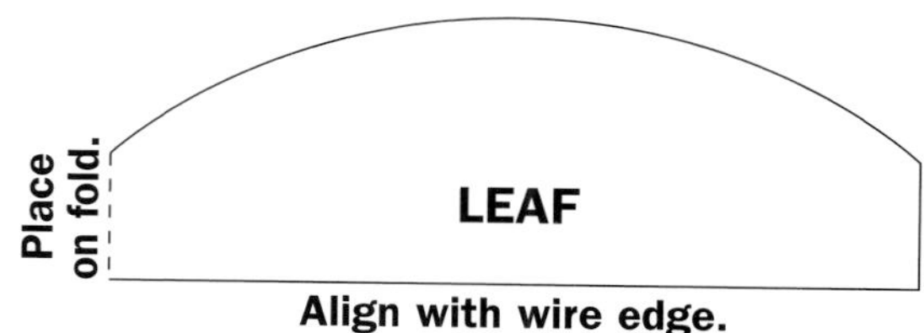

Diagram 3

5. Fold each leaf along seam so that wrong sides are together and wired edges are aligned. Handstitch ⅛" from curved edge, beginning at folded end of ribbon. Before making knot, pull thread to ruffle seam line (see photo). Knot thread to secure. Use fingertips to flatten leaves.

6. To finish, fold and crimp flower edges as desired. Trim ends of stamens on back of flower to make flower lie flat. Tack leaves under flower and tack pin to back of flower.

Three Seasons of Scarves

It's "sew" simple to whip up a fashion sensation with less than a yard of fabric.

Spring Scarf

You will need:

½ yard 54"-wide pink cotton voile
needle and thread to match fabric
sewing machine (optional)
straight pins
72 (4-mm) gold beads
24 each large and small assorted frosted beads

1. For scarf, fold voile in half lengthwise. Using ½" seam allowance, stitch across short ends and along long open edge, leaving 6" opening for turning. To reinforce seam, sew again ⅛" from first seam and ⅜" from raw edges. (Lightweight voile requires this reinforced seam to support beaded edging.) Trim seams, clip corners, and turn. Slipstitch opening closed.

2. For beaded edging, beginning and ending at corners, measure and mark 12 evenly spaced points across each short end of scarf, using straight pins. Secure doubled length of thread to 1 corner of scarf. Thread 1 small gold bead, 1 large frosted bead, 1 small gold bead, 1 small frosted bead, and 1 small gold bead. Pass needle back though small frosted bead and remaining beads in group. Knot to secure thread. Insert needle between layers of fabric and exit at next marked point. Knot thread and add next bead group in same manner as above. Repeat for a total of 12 bead groups on each short end.

Fall Scarf

You will need:

½ yard each 54"-wide crushed velvet: yellow, apple green
thread to match fabrics

1. From each piece of velvet, cut 1 (13"x 54") piece.

2. With right sides facing and raw edges aligned, stitch pieces together, leaving 6"opening for turning. Turn. Slipstitch opening closed.

Winter Scarf

You will need:

Purchased black scarf
3 (9" x 12") sheets felt each: apple green, turquoise, fuchsia
18 (1") yellow buttons
black embroidery floss

1. Transfer flower pattern to felt pieces and cut 6 flowers from each color. Cut out flowers.

2. Position flowers on scarf as desired. Place button in center of each flower. Using black floss, stitch through buttons and all layers to secure flowers to scarf.

Bejeweled Barrettes

Fashion everyday findings into handsome hair-holders.

Beaded Wire Barrette

To ensure that your barrettes will be comfortable, choose lightweight decorations.

You will need:

For each:
4" bow clip barrette
low-temperature glue gun and glue sticks
wire cutters

For beaded wire barrette:
6-mm assorted small glass beads
24-gauge copper wire

For gem barrette:
plastic gems
24-gauge copper wire

For braided barrette:
1/4"-diameter stainless steel pull chain
1/8"-diameter nickel-plated steel pull chain
1/16"-diameter nickel-plated steel pull chain

1. For **beaded wire barrette,** apply glue to section of barrette. Press several beads into glue, leaving holes in beads exposed. Repeat to fully cover barrette, stacking beads if desired. Let dry. Using wire cutters, cut an approximate 6" length of wire. Beginning at 1 end of barrette, insert 1 end of wire into hole of 1 bead, gluing to secure wire end. Let dry.

Thread remaining wire through holes of other beads on barrette, twisting and curling wire as desired (see photo at left). To finish, insert remaining end of wire into hole of 1 bead, gluing to secure. Let dry. If desired, thread multiple lengths of wire through beads.

2. For **braided barrette,** use wire cutters to cut 2 (5") lengths of each pull chain. Using 1 length of each chain, make loose braid. Secure ends with dab of glue. Glue braid to barrette. Let dry. Repeat with remaining lengths of chain to cover barrette. If necessary, trim excess chain from ends of barrette with wire cutters.

3. For **gem barrette,** arrange desired gems on barrette and glue in place. Let dry. Using wire cutters, cut an approximate 10" length of wire. Beginning at 1 end of barrette, crisscross wire between gems to create illusion of jewelry fittings. Glue ends of wire to back of barrette. Let dry.

Stacked-Button Sweater

Bring a cardigan to a fitting close with layers of pearly buttons.

We used mother-of-pearl and abalone shell buttons because of their iridescence.

You will need:

purchased sweater
mother-of-pearl buttons in assorted sizes
abalone shell buttons in assorted sizes
needle and thread to match sweater
4-mm silver beads
3-mm pearl beads
6-mm pearl beads
large snaps (optional)

If the button stack will not fit through the buttonhole, use snaps and attach the stacked buttons through the buttonhole.

1. Remove original buttons from purchased sweater. For front of sweater, stack 2 or 3 buttons as desired, placing smaller buttons on top of larger buttons. (Use original buttons in stack, if desired.) Check to see if stacked buttons will pass through buttonhole. If buttons do not fit through hole, see Step 3.

2. Stitch 1 bottom button to sweater with 1 pass of thread. Place second button on top, aligning holes with bottom button. Bring needle up through both buttons and secure second button with 1 pass of thread. Repeat with third button. To add bead, bring needle up through all buttons and thread 1 silver bead on top of buttons. Secure bead with 2 passes of thread. Knot thread and trim ends. Repeat to add all buttons to front of sweater.

3. If stacked buttons do not fit through buttonholes, stitch each button stack to prong side of 1 snap. Stitch remaining side of snaps to sweater. Snap each button stack into place through 1 buttonhole. Or if neck of sweater is large enough to put on without undoing buttons, stitch button stacks to sweater through buttonholes.

4. For sleeves, stitch on assorted buttons as desired. Referring to Step 2, add 1 or 2 pearl beads on top of some buttons (see photos).

tip

Avoid the frustration of tangled thread by coating your thread with beeswax. Simply pass the thread over a block of beeswax and then iron the thread. Heat from the iron melts the wax into the thread, strengthening it and preventing snarls.

Appliquéd Grapevine Shirt

Add bunches of taste to your wardrobe with this no-sew appliqué.

When appliquéing a small design like this one, choose bright fabrics with a small print so that the colors will stand out.

You will need:

purchased shirt with collar and front pocket
fabric scraps: purple, green
iron-on transfers (See page 147.)
paper
straight pins
fusible web
dimensional paints: purple, green

1. Before transferring design, wash, dry, and iron shirt and fabric scraps. Cut out desired transfer from page 147, leaving as much excess paper around design as possible. Place scrap of paper underneath fabric in case transfer bleeds through.

2. For 1 grapevine motif, place 1 grape bunch transfer facedown on right side of purple fabric scrap. Pin in place. Place 2 leaf transfers facedown on right side of green fabric scrap. Pin in place. Place hot, dry iron on 1 transfer. Do not use steam. Hold iron down for 5 to 10 seconds. Do not slide iron because this might smear design. Repeat until all designs are transferred.

3. Following manufacturer's instructions, fuse web to wrong side of fabric scraps. Cut out grape bunch and leaf shapes along outermost iron-on lines.

4. Remove paper backing from fusible web on grape bunch and leaves. Referring to photo at left, fuse leaves in place onto 1 point of collar. Fuse grape bunch in place, partially overlapping ends of leaves. Repeat steps 2–4 for remaining point of collar and for shirt pocket.

5. Outline grape bunch edges and details, using purple dimensional paint. Let dry. Then outline leaf edges and details with green dimensional paint. Let dry. Referring to photos, add vine to collar and to pocket with green dimensional paint. Let dry.

Outlining the edges of the fabric pieces with dimensional paint will finish the edges and secure them to the shirt.

Ribbon-Laced Vest

Join four ready-made crocheted place mats for a lacy topper.

Standard crocheted place mats will make a vest that corresponds to small and medium adult sizes.

You will need:

4 (13" x 19") purchased crocheted place mats
9 yards 3/8"-wide double-faced ribbon
darning needle
needle and thread to match ribbon and place mats
liquid ravel preventer

1. For back of vest, overlap 1 long edge of 1 place mat with 1 long edge of another place mat, aligning outermost holes in crochet pattern. Using 30" length of ribbon and darning needle, lace place mats together, working in and out of holes in crochet pattern. Keep ribbon flat. To secure ribbon at top center of vest back, turn ribbon under 1/4" and handstitch to wrong side.

2. To secure ribbon at bottom center, form teardrop bow with remaining ribbon. Measure 3" from where ribbon lacing emerges from place mats. Fold ribbon under at this point to form loop; handstitch to secure. Then measure 5" from stitch line. Fold under to form second loop and handstitch to secure. Cut ribbon end at angle (see photos).

3. For each front side of vest, overlap 1 long edge of back joined piece with 1 long edge of 1 place mat, aligning holes in pattern and forming side seam. Using 20" length of ribbon and darning needle and beginning at bottom edge, lace place mats together, stopping 8" from bottom edge. (Leave top half of side seam open for armhole.) To secure, fold ribbon under 1/4" at top and handstitch to wrong side. Referring to Step 2, secure ribbon at bottom with teardrop bow.

4. For shoulders, overlap top edge of front place mats with top edge of back joined piece, aligning holes in pattern and forming shoulder seams. Beginning at 1 shoulder edge, use 46" length of ribbon and darning needle to lace place mats together. Lace only half of front place mat to back. (Unlaced sections of front place mats will fold down to form collar.) Continue lacing along top edge of back piece and then attach half of remaining front place mat. Referring to Step 2, secure ribbon at each shoulder with teardrop bow.

5. To maintain vest shape, handstitch all seam ends. Apply liquid ravel preventer to raw ends of each teardrop bow. Let dry.

6. Use remaining ribbon to add decoration. Beginning at 1 underarm seam, lace ribbon up and around edges of 1 front side. Continue lacing across bottom of vest back and around to remaining front side. Lace up and around edges of front side and around underarm to back. Lace up and across top of vest back (under previous lacing) and down to finish at beginning underarm seam. Trim excess ribbon, fold under, and stitch to secure. If desired, use 20" length ribbon to tie vest front (see photo at left).

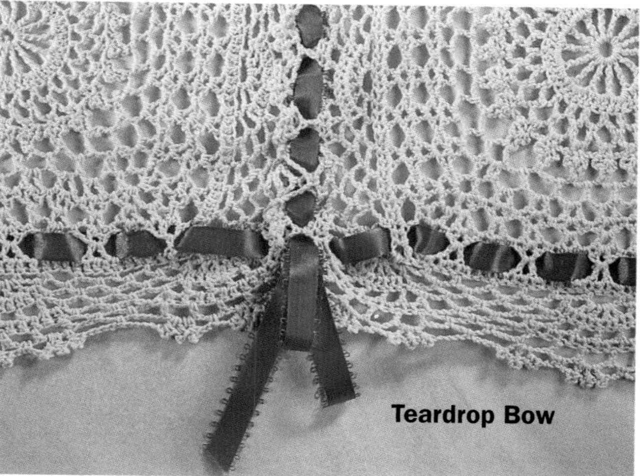

For teardrop bow, measure 3" from end of lacing. Fold ribbon under to form loop and stitch to secure. Then measure 5" from stitch line. Fold under to form second loop and stitch to secure.

Craft Clay Pendants

Add panache to plain outfits with these chic accessories.

You will need (for each):

Promat® modeling compound: Ivory, Pearlescent Silver, Pearlescent Gold
Granitex® modeling compound: Black
parchment paper
rolling pin
round cookie cutters: 2"-diameter, 1½"-diameter
½"-diameter bottle cap
craft knife
¼"-diameter bamboo skewers
drinking glass with flat bottom
blunt-tipped darning needle
glass baking dish
clear acrylic spray sealer (optional)
1¼ yards 2-mm round black leather lacing or 2-mm ivory rattail cord

1. Cover work surface with piece of parchment paper. To soften craft clay, pinch off clay piece and hold it in fist for a few minutes until it begins to soften. Further soften clay piece by rolling it into balls and ropes.

2. For **large disc,** soften ½-ounce piece of clay in desired color; for **small disc,** soften ⅜-ounce piece of clay in desired color. For each piece, cover clay with paper and flatten to ¼" thickness, using rolling pin. Remove paper. Use 2"-diameter cookie cutter to cut out large disc and 1½"-diameter cookie cutter to cut out small disc. Use bottle cap to cut out center of large or small disc. Using fingertips, smooth outside and inside edges on front and back of disc.

3. For **rectangular pendant,** soften ½-ounce piece of clay in desired color. Referring to Step 2, flatten clay to ¼" thickness. Using craft knife, cut out 1⅛" x 2¼" piece. Use bottle cap to cut out hole at 1 end of rectangular piece (see photo at left). Using fingertips, smooth outside and inside edges on front and back of rectangle.

4. For each **round bead,** soften ¼-ounce piece of clay in desired color. For **stonelike bead,** use Granitex clay. Roll clay into ball. For hole in center of bead, insert and twist pointed tip of skewer through clay; remove skewer. From opposite side of bead, twist skewer back through resulting hole; remove skewer.

For **flat bead,** place round bead on paper surface with hole faceup. Cover bead with paper and flatten bead with bottom of glass. Remove paper and reshape hole, using skewer. For **flat irregular bead,** press round bead into palm of hand. Reshape hole, using skewer.

5. To decorate pieces, carve designs into clay, using needle or skewer (see photo at left). For fine lines, use blunt tip of needle. For tiny dots, twist eye end of needle into clay. For large dots, twist end of skewer into clay. For studs, use tiny balls of same type clay to press onto surface of disc or bead.

6. Place finished pieces on paper in baking dish. Following manufacturer's instructions, bake pieces in oven. Remove and let cool. If desired, spray pearlescent pieces with acrylic sealer to increase luster. Let dry.

7. To string disc or pendant, fold 1¼ yards of leather or cord in half. Working from front to back, insert resulting loop through hole in disc or pendant. Slip ends of lacing through loop and pull firmly. To string beads, slip ends of lacing through hole in each desired bead. If desired, knot both halves of lacing together between or above beads (see photo at left). To finish, knot ends of lacing together at desired length.

tip

To flatten the clay to an even thickness, place 2 skewers on each side of the clay piece. Roll the rolling pin perpendicularly along the skewers.

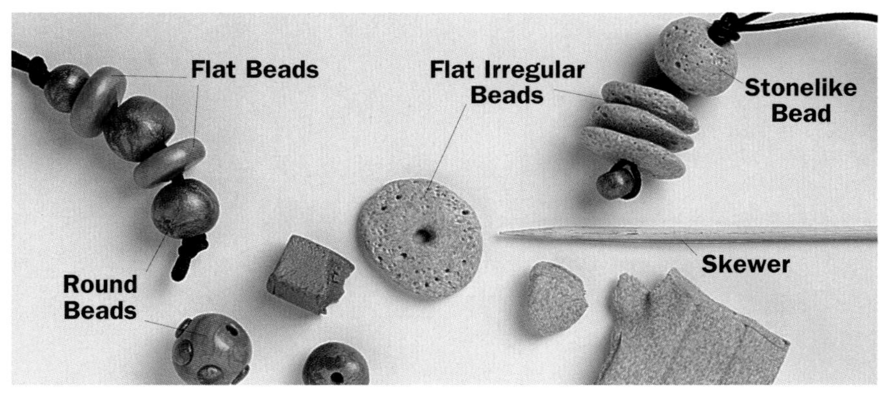

Charming Belt

Layer charms on a plain belt buckle for an easy-to-make fashion statement.

If you prefer gold accessories, decorate a brass belt buckle with antique gold charms.

You will need:

belt with large plain silver buckle (We used a belt with a 3" square buckle.)
assorted antique silver charms (We used approximately 24 charms.)
clear household cement

1. Select charms to cover buckle. If desired, trace outline of buckle on scrap paper and sketch placement of charms on traced buckle. Be sure charms do not project to inside of buckle; belt must be able to pass through buckle (see photos).

2. Using dab of household cement, layer charms on buckle, beginning with flat charms (see photos). Let dry.

Choose a belt with a large plain buckle. Extend the charms over the buckle's outside edges to give the buckle an interesting shape.

tip

Nail polish remover will dissolve the cement and remove the glued charms from the buckle. Dab the glued charms with a cotton ball saturated with remover. Let the remover sit on the surface for a few minutes. Then carefully pry off the charms, using needlenose pliers. If necessary, chip away the dried glue from the buckle, using a craft knife.

Home Front

A few simple techniques yield handmade accents that will warm your home. Even if you think you can't paint, you'll find it a cinch to create luxurious linens with a grapevine stencil. Adding a faux finish to plain watering cans can turn watering your plants into pleasure. Give plain pillowcases that designer look with borders fashioned from fabric, ribbon, and buttons. Make an easy-to-sew throw trimmed with handmade tassels and wrap yourself in elegance.

page 52
page 60
page 66
page 56

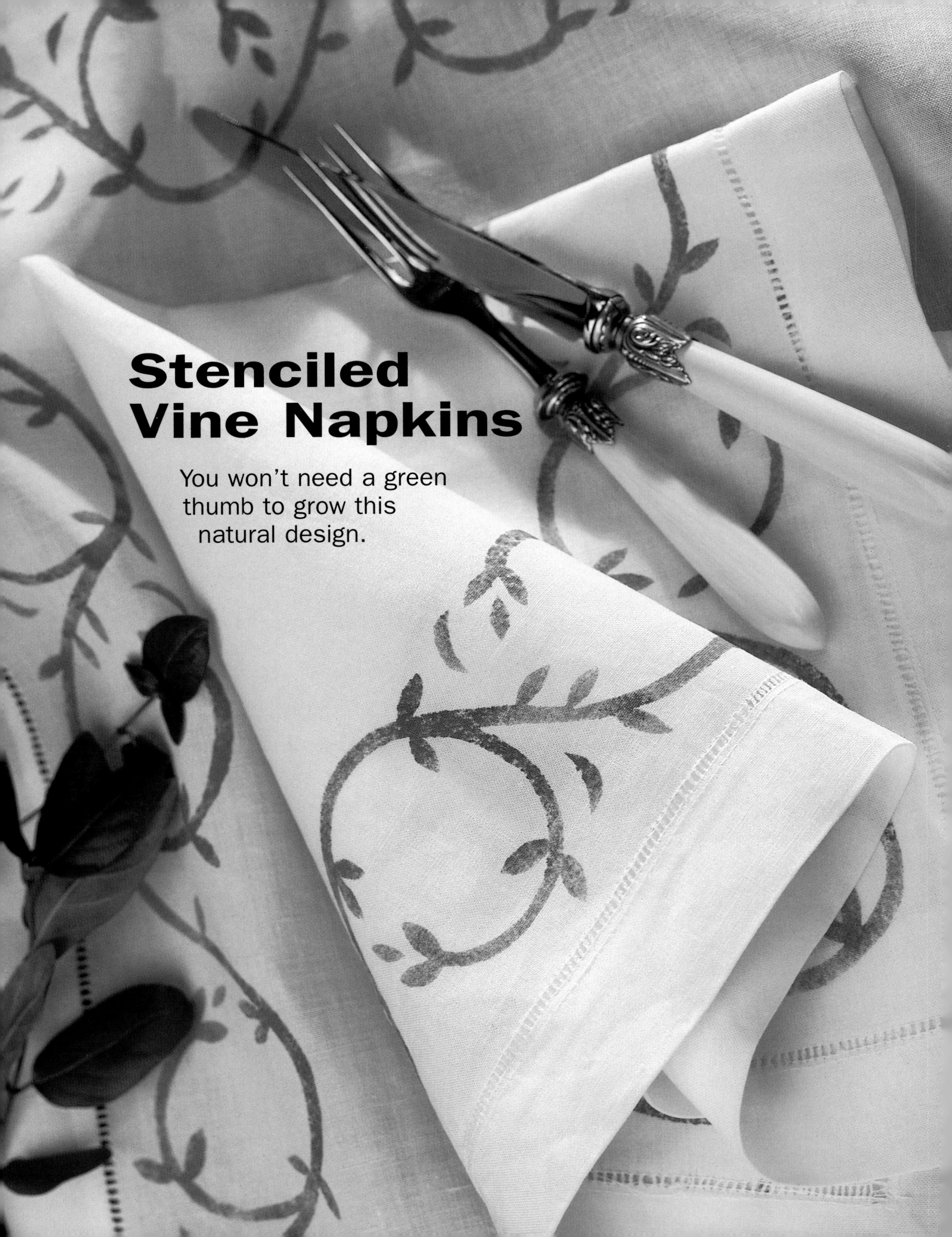

Stenciled Vine Napkins

You won't need a green thumb to grow this natural design.

You will need (for each):

22"-square linen or cotton napkin (A 1" hem-stitched border is optional.)
vine stencil pattern (See page 149.)
8 ½" x 11" sheet plastic template material
black marker
protective mat or cardboard
craft knife
masking tape
green acrylic paint (We used Delta Ceramcoat Leaf Green.)
acrylic textile medium
small stencil brush
pressing cloth
iron

1. Wash and dry napkin; do not use fabric softener in washer or dryer. Iron napkin without starch to provide smooth, clean surface for stenciling.

2. Trace stencil pattern onto frosted side of plastic using marker. Place stencil pattern on protective mat. Using craft knife, cut out stencil, starting with buds and leaves. When cutting out leaves, pull knife from tip of leaf to stem.

3. Tape napkin onto clean work surface. Place stencil in lower right corner of napkin, 1½" from bottom edge (or ½" from hemstitched border). Tape stencil in place.

4. Mix equal parts paint and textile medium. Dip dry brush into paint. Dab brush onto scrap of paper to remove excess paint. Holding brush perpendicular to napkin, lightly pounce brush onto fabric to stencil design. Carefully lift stencil. Reposition and repeat to stencil remaining corners **(Diagram 1).** Let dry. On 1 side of napkin, position stencil between finished motifs to complete vine design **(Diagram 1).**

Diagram 1

5. If center motif does not touch previously stenciled designs at each end, once paint is dry, reposition stencil and paint end to complete vine **(Diagram 2).** Repeat steps 4 and 5 on remaining sides to make continuous pattern around napkin.

Diagram 2

6. Using pressing cloth and dry iron on medium setting, press napkin to heat-set paint.

Once you've stenciled a motif in each corner, position the stencil on one side of napkin between two motifs. Stencil design to make a continuous vine pattern.

tip

As you practice stenciling on a fabric scrap before beginning your project, note how much paint you load onto the brush and how heavily you pounce the paint onto the fabric. Become comfortable with your technique to achieve consistent results.

Tabletop Topiaries

These tiny trees are the right height for comment-worthy centerpieces.

Star Tree

Rose Globe

Topiary Base

You will need:

1 block florist's foam or 1 package plaster of Paris for base
1 small terra-cotta pot
hot-glue gun and glue sticks
1 stick (Length will vary according to desired height of topiary.)
duct tape or other heavy-duty tape (for plaster of Paris base)
Spanish moss or sheet moss

1. You can make either a foam base or plaster base to suit your needs. (A plaster base will be more sturdy and permanent.) For **florist's foam base**, cut foam to fit snugly in pot. Press firmly into pot. Cover 1 end of stick with hot glue. Anchor glue-covered end of stick into foam.

For **plaster of Paris base**, cover drainage hole at bottom of pot, using tape. Following manufacturer's instructions, fill pot with plaster of Paris to within 1" of top. While plaster is setting, insert stick into pot. To secure stick while plaster dries, place length of tape over mouth of pot on both sides of stick. Let dry.

2. Hot-glue moss to foam or plaster base to cover.

Star Tree

You will need:

topiary base (See **Topiary Base** above.)
1 (9"-tall) Styrofoam cone
hot-glue gun and glue sticks
natural-colored twisted paper roll
40 small wooden star cutouts
Spanish moss
½"-wide gold wire-edged ribbon
raffia

Note: Finished tree is approximately 15" tall.

1. Insert stick of topiary base into bottom of cone. Secure with a little hot glue.

2. Untwist twisted paper and flatten. Starting at bottom of cone and wrapping upward, hot-glue flattened paper to cone to cover. Glue star cutouts to cone as desired, reserving 1 star for top of tree. Glue small tuft of Spanish moss below top star (see photo). Handling gold ribbon and raffia as 1, tie bow around rim of pot.

3. To add sparkle to topiary, spray stars gold before gluing them to tree. Or for a Christmas tree, glue green paper to Styrofoam base and accent with stars you've painted red.

Rose Globe

You will need:

topiary base (See **Topiary Base** above.)
1 (4"-diameter) Styrofoam ball
hot-glue gun and glue sticks
dried rose petals (We used petals from 10 large roses.)
gold crinkle wire

Note: Finished topiary is approximately 9" tall.

1. Insert stick of topiary base into ball. Secure with a little hot glue.

2. Hot-glue dried rose petals to ball to cover. Referring to photo, wrap crinkle wire around ball.

Save money by drying your own rose petals. Place 3 paper towels on a microwave-safe plate. Arrange a single layer of fresh petals on top of the paper towels. Cover with a single paper towel. Microwave on HIGH for 3 minutes, periodically replacing moist paper towels with dry ones. Check the petals for dryness. They should be dry but not so brittle that they crumble when picked up. If necessary, continue microwaving at 30-second intervals, checking for desired dryness.

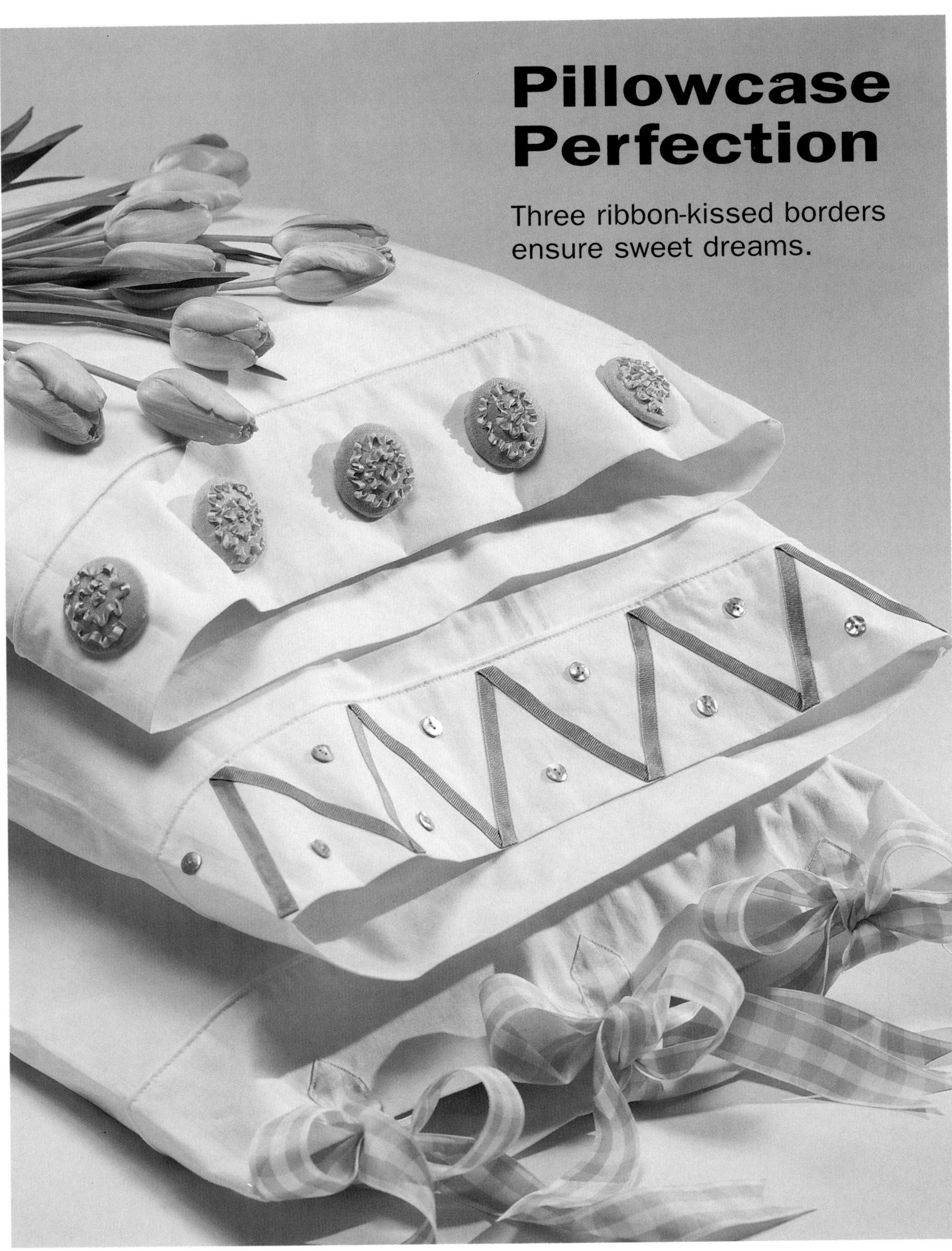

Pillowcase Perfection

Three ribbon-kissed borders ensure sweet dreams.

You will need:

For each:
1 standard pillowcase with piped edge along cuff
needle and thread to match ribbon and pillowcase

Button Edging:
5 (1⅞") half-dome covered button forms
⅛ yard lightweight fabric
2½ yards 4-mm silk ribbon

Zigzag Edging:
straight pins
1½ yards ⅜"-wide grosgrain ribbon
flexible fabric glue
11 (⅜") mother-of-pearl buttons

Bow Edging:
straight pins
3½ yards 1⅛"-wide gingham ribbon
sewing machine (optional)
liquid ravel preventer

Button Edging

1. Using pattern on back of covered button package, trace and cut out 5 circles from fabric. For ribbon spiral pattern, trace circle onto paper. Draw loose spiral in center of circle.

2. Stack 1 fabric circle on top of pattern and place against windowpane. Transfer spiral pattern to fabric, using pencil. Repeat with all fabric circles.

3. From ribbon, cut 5 (18") pieces. Thread needle with thread to match ribbon. For each circle, turn 1 end of 1 ribbon under and stitch at center of spiral. Stitch ribbon in spiral, securing at ¼" intervals. Between stitches, scoot ribbon up a little to make small wave and then stitch (see photo below). Continue to anchor ribbon along marked spiral. Trim ribbon ⅛" from end of spiral. Fold ribbon end under ⅛" and stitch to anchor.

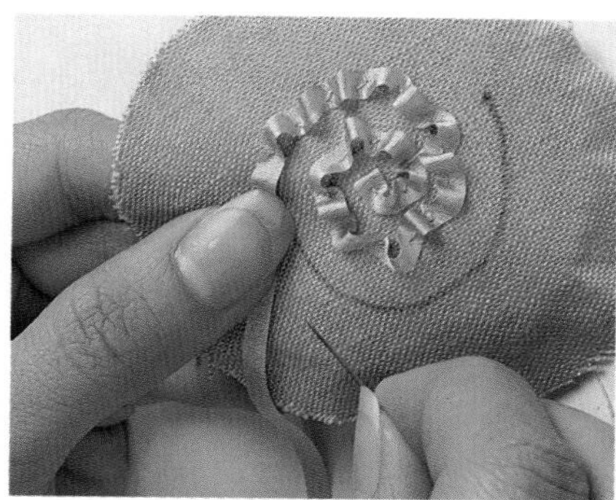

4. Following manufacturer's instructions, cover buttons with finished circles.

5. Evenly space buttons along 1 side of cuff. Stitch in place with thread to match pillowcase.

Zigzag Edging

1. Measure width of pillowcase and divide into 5 equal segments. Beginning and ending at corners, mark these segments along bottom edge of cuff, using straight pins. Measure and mark 5 midpoints along piped edge of cuff **(Zigzag Edging Diagram).** (For standard pillowcase, segments will be 4".)

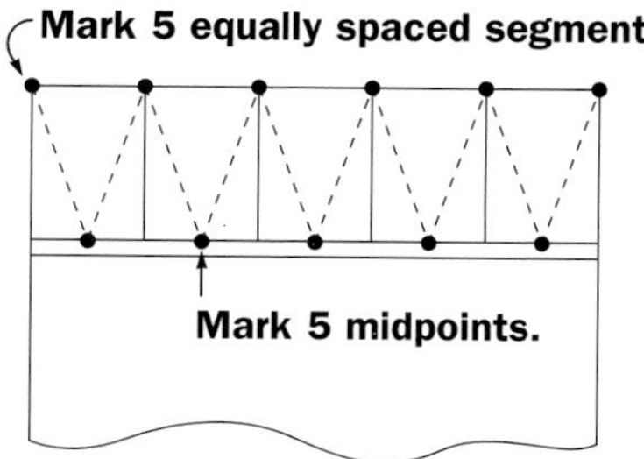

Zigzag Edging Diagram

2. Turn 1 cut end of ribbon under ¼" and glue. Beginning and ending in 1 corner at bottom edge, fold and glue ribbon in large zigzag between marked points. Trim ribbon ¼" from end point. Fold ribbon end under ¼" and glue. Tack ribbon points with small stitches for added stability.

3. Center buttons between points, approximately 1" from piped and outer edges (see photo on opposite page). Stitch in place.

Bow Edging

1. Measure and mark 3 equally spaced points along front and back edge of pillowcase, using straight pins. (For standard pillowcase cuff, points are approximately 7" apart.)

2. Cut ribbon into 6 (21") lengths. Turn under 1 end of 1 ribbon to form a point and pin to cuff at 1 marked point (see photo on opposite page). Overlap end of ribbon 1½" over cuff of pillowcase; remainder will be used to tie bow. Stitch ribbon in place, ⅛" from ribbon edge. Remove pin.

3. Repeat Step 2 to stitch 5 remaining ribbons in place to make 3 sets of ribbon ties along pillowcase opening.

4. Trim loose ends of ribbons into V shape. Apply liquid ravel preventer to cut ends. Insert pillow and tie ribbons into bows.

Lace and Raffia Cover-up

For a simple slipcover, drape a lace curtain over a chair and tie with raffia tassels.

This slipcover is pretty but temporary. Use it for special dinners or parties.

You will need:

small roll of raffia
1 (44" x 96") polyester lace curtain panel
chair

1. For medium-sized raffia tassel, use approximately 18 (20"-long) strands of raffia. For larger tassel, use more strands. Form strands into 6"-diameter circle. Loop 2 more strands through circle and tie in knot **(Photo 1).** The loose strands will form tassel tie.

2. Press sides of circle together. Using several more raffia strands, wrap and bind circle approximately 1" below knot **(Photo 2).** After wrapping strands around circle several times, tie strands in knot. Trim excess. To complete tassel, cut looped strands of circle opposite tassel tie. Trim to neaten.

3. To make raffia cord for securing lace around chair, use approximately 12 (48"-long) strands of raffia. To attach tassels to raffia cord, knot each end of raffia cord to tassel tie of 1 tassel.

4. Referring to photo at left, drape chair with lace. Wrap raffia cord around base of chair back and tie in knot in back, letting tassel ends dangle. If desired, tie additional tassels onto knot in back **(Photo 3).**

tip

If you prefer a colorful look for your raffia tassels, mix colored strands of twine, jute, or cording in with the raffia. In the same vein, you could glue beads, seashells, or buttons to the binding of your tassel.

Photo 1

Photo 2

Photo 3

Color-Washed Watering Cans

With their fresh faux finish, these pretty cans should stay in view to remind you to water your plants.

Verdigris Watering Can

Verdigris Watering Can

You will need:

tin watering can
Anita's™ Faux Easy Copper Base Coat
Anita's™ Faux Easy Glaze: Verdigris, White
Anita's™ Polyurethane Satin Varnish
paintbrush
sea sponge

1. Using paintbrush, apply 2 base coats of copper to can, letting dry after each application.

2. Moisten sponge and squeeze out excess water. Dip sponge into verdigris glaze, squeezing sponge to distribute glaze. While tilting can, randomly sponge on verdigris glaze. Dip sponge in water and dab over wet glaze, letting glaze drip down side of tilted can (see photo at left).

3. For highlight, mix verdigris glaze with white glaze to make lighter shade of verdigris. Dip sponge into highlight glaze and lightly sponge over wet verdigris glaze (see photo at left). Dip sponge in water again and dab over wet glazes, letting glazes drip down side of tilted can. Let dry.

4. To finish, apply 1 coat of varnish to can with paintbrush. Let dry.

Antiqued Watering Can

Antiqued Watering Can

You will need:

tin watering can
Anita's™ Faux Easy Ecru Base Coat
Anita's™ Faux Easy Dark Brown Glaze
Anita's™ Polyurethane Satin Varnish
paintbrush
sponge brush
cotton rag
old toothbrush

1. Using paintbrush, apply 2 base coats of ecru to can, letting dry after each application.

2. Using sponge brush, sponge over base coat with liberal amount of dark brown glaze.

3. Moisten rag and squeeze out excess water. Use rag to remove glaze, wiping toward top and bottom edges of can. Let glaze collect in crevices of can. Remove as much or as little glaze as necessary to achieve desired antiqued look (see photo below). Let dry.

4. Using toothbrush, flyspeck can with glaze. To flyspeck, hold toothbrush with bristles angled toward can. Run your thumb over bristles, letting small specks of glaze hit can (see photo below). Let dry.

5. To finish, apply 1 coat of varnish to can with paintbrush. Let dry.

Antiquing is a great painting technique for items with interesting shapes. The dark brown glaze gathers in crevices, accentuating the details. Try antiquing with a different color base coat—consider yellow, red, or green.

Fragrant Swag

Preserve the herbs of summer with a dried remembrance that smells as sweet as a country afternoon.

In the wintertime, hang this swag from your mantel and clip off a bundle to toss in the fire.

You will need:

3 purchased dried pomegranates
electric drill with ⅛" bit
2½ yards jute string or twine
fresh-cut fragrant herbs (We suggest artemisia, oregano, rosemary, sage, scented geranium, and/or thyme.)
fresh-cut flowers or blooming herbs (We used lamb's ears, marigold, and Mexican sage.)
large-eyed tapestry needle

1. Drill hole from top to bottom through center of each pomegranate. Set aside. Cut 4 (6") lengths of jute string or twine. Set aside.

2. Gather desired herbs into 2½"-diameter bundle. For color, center flowers in front of bundle. Wrap 1 (6") length of string very tightly around bundle; knot to secure. Trim ends of string close to knot. Repeat to make 3 more bundles.

3. Cut 1½ yards of string. Thread needle with doubled strand of string and knot at 1 end. Thread pomegranates on string, leaving 5" at knotted end below bottom pomegranate, approximately 5" between remaining pomegranates, and 5" above top pomegranate. Cut string at top 5" mark. Remove needle.

4. Insert herb bundles between doubled strands of string below, between, and on top of pomegranates (see photo at left). Pull free ends of string to tighten. Tie knot above top bundle to secure. Knot ends of string together to make hanger.

5. To use as fireplace scent, clip 1 herb bundle, reserving pomegranate. Using fireplace tools, carefully place bundle onto fire in fireplace. Secure remaining bundles with knot. Save pomegranates for another use; do not place them in fire.

Make an almost-instant swag for your kitchen. Tuck bundles of herbs and hot peppers into a purchased raffia braid. Pinch them off as needed for cooking.

Hand-painted Sisal Rug

With tape and spray paint, an ordinary rug acquires designer-look cachet.

The masking tape acts like a stencil, covering the areas on the rug you do not want painted.

You will need:

newspaper
purchased sisal rug with binding (We used a 24" x 36" rug.)
freezer paper
masking tape: 1"-wide, 2"-wide
dark brown spray paint
clear acrylic spray sealer

Photo 1

Photo 2

1. To protect work surface, cover surface with newspaper.

2. Cut 12" x 24" rectangle from freezer paper to cover center of rug. Place rectangle, shiny side down, in center of rug. Secure edges with 2"-wide tape.

3. To create border design on rug, use tape to cover areas of rug you do not want painted. Around entire rug, use 1"-wide tape to cover strip adjacent to binding. Leave binding uncovered. Around entire rug, use 2"-wide tape to cover strip between rectangle and tape adjacent to binding.

4. To create checked design, use pieces of 1"-wide tape to cover areas between 2"-wide strip of tape and rectangle, leaving tiny squares between each piece.

5. Before painting rug, be sure tape is completely covering all desired areas. Then spray-paint all uncovered areas of rug, including binding **(Photo 1).** Spray over tape to ensure uncovered areas will be thoroughly painted. Let dry.

6. Carefully remove tape and rectangle from rug **(Photo 2).** To finish, spray rug with acrylic sealer. Let dry.

Showers of Flowers Throw

Trimmed with handmade tassels, this elegant accent is simple to sew.

Because the batting is caught in the seam line, you won't need to bother with quilting.

You will need:

1½ yards each 54"-wide fabric: floral print, solid (We used matelassé for solid fabric.)
1½ yards 54"-wide thin polyester batting
straight pins
needle and thread to match fabrics
sewing machine
4 yards 4"-long decorator fringe to match fabrics
low-temperature glue gun and glue sticks
4 (1"-diameter) wooden beads
acrylic paint (optional)
paintbrush (optional)

1. Aligning raw edges, pin print fabric to batting. Using needle and thread, hand-baste print fabric to batting 1" from each edge.

2. For each tassel, cut 1 yard of fringe. Fold 1 piece of fringe back over braid for hanger **(Photo 1).** To form tassel, tightly roll fringe around hanger piece, applying glue to braid of fringe as you roll **(Photo 1).** While rolling fringe, gradually spiral top edge of braid downward to form cone. Continue rolling until you reach end of fringe, securing end with hot-glue. Let dry.

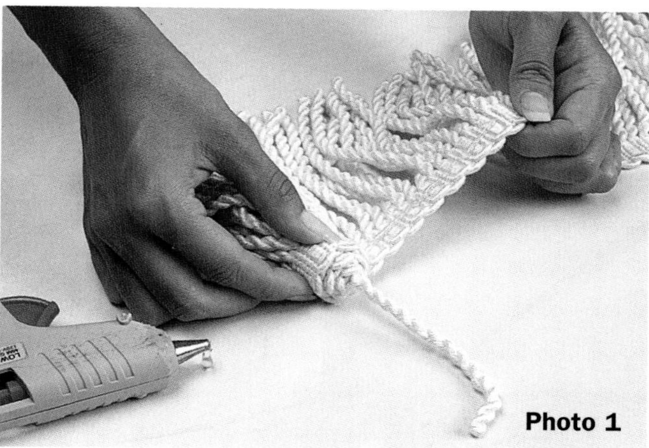

Photo 1

3. If desired, paint beads with acrylic paints to coordinate. Let dry. Thread 1 bead onto hanger of each tassel **(Photo 2).**

Photo 2

4. Position 1 tassel at each corner on right side of solid fabric, with tassel ends toward center of fabric square and tassel hangers in seam allowances. Pin and then baste tassels in place.

5. With right sides facing and raw edges aligned, pin solid and print-and-batting squares together, making sure tassel ends are free of seam allowances. Using ½" seam allowance, stitch around all edges, removing pins as you work and leaving 12" opening on 1 side of square.

6. Turn throw to right side through opening. Press seams flat. Slipstitch opening closed. Topstitch 1" from finished edges.

tip

Use a zipper foot on your sewing machine to ease sewing over the tassels. And to make sewing through multiple layers of fabric easier, lengthen the machine stitch.

Coffee-Lover's Apron

Brew up creative kitchen-wear with the designs on page 151.

For a matching accessory, iron a coffee cup design onto a plain white oven mitt or potholder. Paint the design with bright fabric paints.

You will need:

apron
iron-on transfers (See page 151.)
paper
straight pins
textile medium
acrylic paints: yellow, red, purple, turquoise, fuchsia, green
soft bristle paintbrush
black permanent fabric marker
black dimensional fabric paint

1. Before transferring designs, wash, dry, and iron apron. Do not use fabric softener in washer or dryer. Cut out each transfer from page 151, leaving as much excess paper around each as possible. Place piece of paper underneath apron front to prevent transfers from bleeding through.

2. Referring to photo at left, place each transfer facedown on right side of apron. Pin each in place. Place hot, dry iron on 1 transfer. Do not use steam. Hold iron down for 5 to 10 seconds. Do not slide iron because this may smear design. Repeat until all designs are transferred.

3. To paint designs, for each color, mix equal parts paint and textile medium. Referring to photo at left, paint designs. Let paint dry between colors and coats. (We used 2 coats on most areas of each design.)

4. Referring to photo at left, outline diamonds on red cup, circles on white cup, and flower petals on green cup, using fabric marker. Outline remaining details on each design, using dimensional paint. Following paint manufacturer's directions, let dry completely before washing.

Outline the circles, using a black permanent fabric marker. Outline the remaining details, including the solid black dots, with black dimensional paint (see Step 4).

Playful Pansy Lampshade

Light your room with the colors of pressed pansies.

We used fiber-speckled handmade paper to add texture to the shade surface.

You will need:

smooth fabric or plastic lampshade
posterboard
handmade paper or tissue paper
fusible web
dried pansies
small pillow (optional)
low-temperature glue gun and glue sticks

1. To make lampshade pattern, place seam side of shade down onto posterboard. Make mark on posterboard at seam line of shade. Then roll shade along posterboard, marking bottom edge of shade as you roll **(Photo 1).** Stop rolling when seam of shade is again down on posterboard. At this point, make mark on posterboard at seam line. Roll shade back to starting point. In same manner, mark top edge of shade, making sure bottom edge of shade follows previously marked line.

2. Cut out pattern, adding 1" each to top and bottom edges of shade. Cut out 1 pattern each from handmade paper and fusible web. From remaining fusible web, cut small circle to cover each pansy.

3. Using iron on medium setting, iron fusible web pattern onto paper pattern. Remove paper backing from fusible web. Place pansies facedown onto fusible web as desired. Iron 1 fusible web circle over each pansy and remove paper backing **(Photo 2).**

4. Carefully position pansy-covered paper over shade, butting ends of paper at seam of shade. Using iron on medium setting and beginning at ends of paper, fuse paper to shade **(Photo 3).** If desired, place small pillow inside shade to steady shade while ironing. Iron over paper until it is completely bonded to shade.

5. To finish, hot-glue 1" paper overlap at top and bottom edges of shade to inside of shade. Let dry.

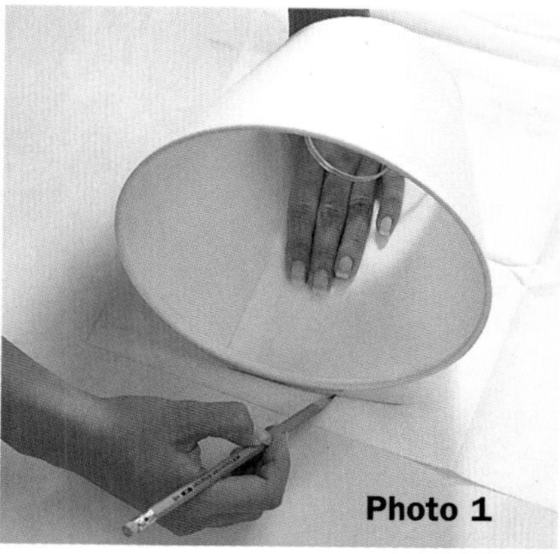
Photo 1

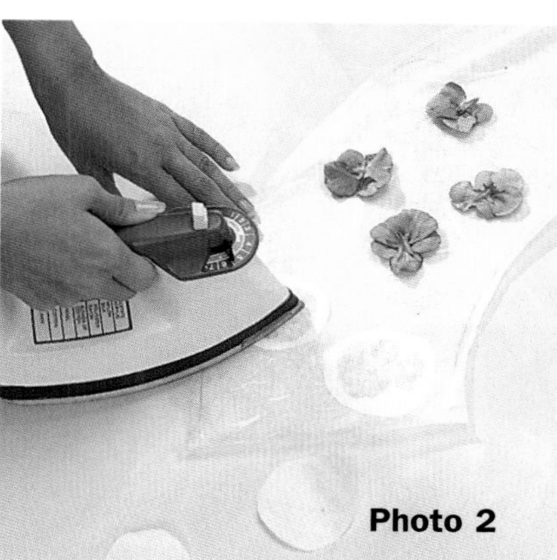
Photo 2

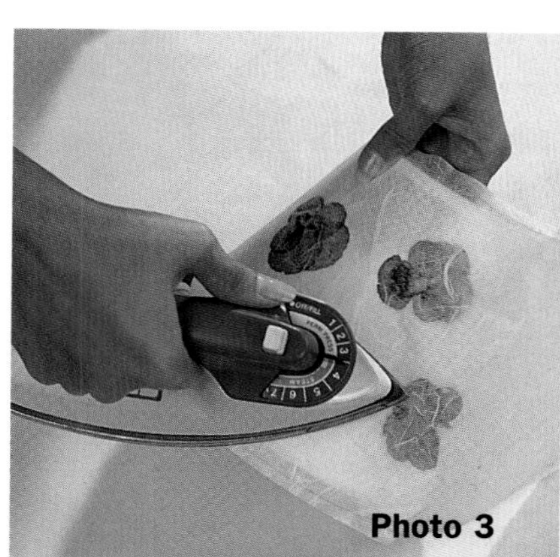
Photo 3

Craft Batches

From church bazaars to party favors, here are some great ideas for those times you have to craft a lot of projects fast. Start by doodling simple designs on glass plates and white chargers. Then tuck potpourri inside organza squares for pretty sachets. Cut out cherub prints to make cards and picture frames with that celestial air. And have fun in the kitchen making sunflower napkin rings using items from your pantry.

page 90
page 88
page 82
page 78

Decoupage Pots

This French cut-and-paste craft translates ordinary flowerpots into ooh-la-la.

You will need (for each):

4" clay pot (We used a rose pot for each, which is taller and narrower than a standard pot.)
acrylic spray sealant
acrylic paints: for **fish pot,** bright blue, turquoise, and silver metallic; for **angel pot,** bright magenta, white, bright red, and antique gold; for **baby pot,** light green and white
sponge
1" paintbrush
paper cutouts from magazines, catalogs, or wrapping paper to complement theme
Mod Podge (gloss finish)
400 grit sandpaper
assorted novelties to complement theme (optional)
hot-glue gun and glue sticks (optional)

1. To make pot easier to paint, spray inside and out with sealant. Let dry.

2. To paint **fish pot**, sponge-paint alternate blue and turquoise vertical stripes on pot. Let dry. Paint over with silver. Let dry. To paint **angel pot**, combine 1 part magenta, 1 part white, and ½ part red. Apply 2 coats to pot, letting dry between applications. Paint gold stripes around rim. Let dry. To paint **baby pot**, combine equal parts light green and white. Apply 2 coats to pot, letting dry between applications. For **each pot**, paint inside if desired. Let dry.

3. To glue on each cutout, coat back with Mod Podge. Press onto pot, being careful to smooth out any wrinkles. Continue to add cutouts until desired effect is achieved. Let dry.

4. Apply 5 coats of Mod Podge to all painted surfaces of pot, letting dry slightly between applications. When fifth coat is dry, lightly sand pot with wet sandpaper. Apply 3 more coats of Mod Podge. Let dry.

5. If desired, hot-glue novelties around rim of pot (see photo at left). Let dry.

You can cut out decoupage designs from magazines, catalogs, or wrapping paper.

Funny Face Pins

Making and wearing these comic creations will surely bring a smile.

CAT

GIRL

BOY

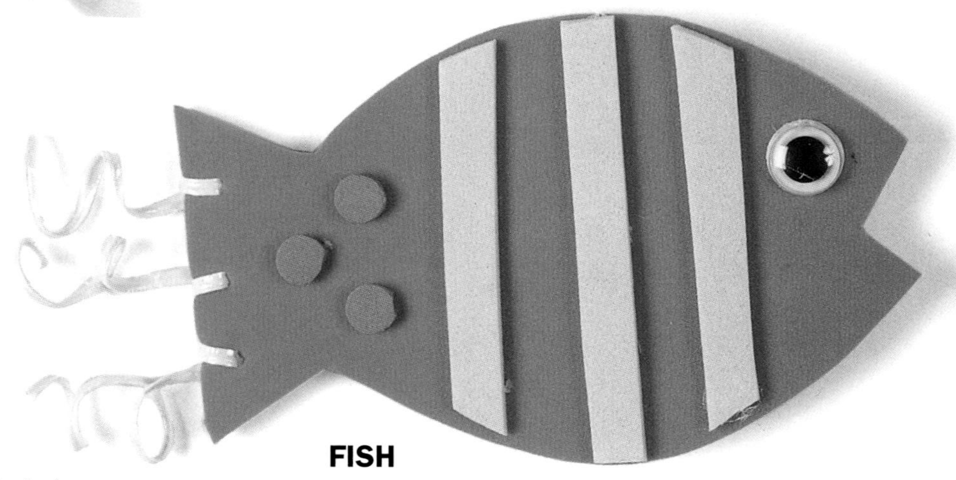

FISH

Designs are actual size.

You will need (for 4 pins):

tracing paper
1 (9" x 12") sheet each craft foam: yellow, purple, green, bright pink, peach
¼" hole punch
wiggle eyes: 2 (7-mm) each for boy, girl, and cat pin; 1 (10-mm) for fish pin
bendable ribbon or craft wire: yellow, green, white
hot-glue gun and glue sticks
4 (1") pin backs

1. Using tracing paper, trace patterns from photos at left. Transfer patterns to colors of foam indicated. Cut out, using ¼" hole punch to make holes for bendable ribbon. Reserve "polka dots" from holes.

2. Referring to photos, glue shapes and eyes to bases.

3. From color of bendable ribbon indicated, cut following lengths: 4 (6") for boy, 6 (6") for girl, 6 (4") for cat, and 3 (4") for fish. For each pin, referring to photos and working from back, pierce foam ¼" from edge with ribbons. Push each length through ½" to front. Bend ribbons over edge to back. To shape ribbons, bend into zigzags or curl around pencil.

4. Hot-glue 1 pin back to back of each shape.

Pin all these colorful companions on a T-shirt or pin one on a jacket lapel.

Angelic Accents

Cut out cherub prints and craft these heavenly mementos.

Ribbon-and-Angels Frame

Heart-and-Angels Card

Flying Angel Card

You will need:

For each:
craft glue
desired angel cutout (See page 153.)

For heart-and-angels card:
assorted textured papers or tissue paper
purchased plain note card
1/8"-wide satin ribbon

For flying angel card:
light blue artist's paper or construction paper
white textured paper or tissue paper
colored pencils
star punch
hole punch
1/4"-wide satin ribbon

For ribbon-and-angels frame:
artist's paper
precut mat-board frame
1/2"-wide wire-edged ribbon
hot-glue gun and glue sticks

1. Referring to photo at left for desired project, cut out design from page 153 or copy design on photocopier and then cut out. If using photocopier, enlarge or reduce design as desired.

2. For **heart-and-angels card,** tear heart and square from different colors of textured paper. Glue paper shapes onto front of purchased note card (see photo at left). Let dry. Glue cutout angels and ribbon onto paper heart, slipping ribbon underneath 1 angel and up through opening in middle of angels. Secure ribbon at desired points with dots of craft glue (see photo at left). Let dry.

3. For **flying angel card,** cut artist's paper to desired size. Then cut textured paper approximately 1/2" smaller on all sides. Color cutout angel with colored pencils. Glue angel onto textured paper (see photo at left). Use star punch to punch out stars as desired from textured paper and remaining artist's paper. Glue blue stars onto white paper, positioning stars around angel on front of card (see photo at left). Glue white stars onto blue paper. Let dry.

Position textured paper on top of artist's paper. Using hole punch, punch holes through both layers, 1/2" from edge. Attach pieces by folding ribbon through holes (see photo at left).

4. For **ribbon-and-angels frame,** glue cutout angels onto piece of artist's paper with craft glue. Let dry. Cut out angels from artist's paper. (Attaching angels to artist's paper makes angels sturdy enough to extend above edge of frame.) Using craft glue, glue angels onto top edge of frame, letting top half of angels extend above edge of frame (see photo at left). Loop wire-edged ribbon 4 times. Pinch loop together in center and tie with long piece of ribbon to make bow (see photo at left). Using hot glue, attach bow to back of angels, dangling tails of ribbon over front of frame (see photo at left). Let dry. To curl ribbon, wrap ribbon tails around pencil.

Use a star punch to cut out stars from the papers. The opened card reveals the white stars glued to the inside.

Faux-Leather Boxes

With this simple leather-look painting technique, you can decorate a stack of keepsake boxes.

For a different faux-leather look, use red, yellow, or light brown paint as a base coat under the antiquing medium.

You will need (for each):

papier-mâché box
FolkArt acrylic paints: Kelly Green #407, Pure Gold #660
paintbrushes
FolkArt antiquing medium: Woodn' Bucket Brown #817
plastic wrap
sponge
Royal Coat Press & Peel Foil Kit #1422
FolkArt Matte-Acrylic Sealer #788

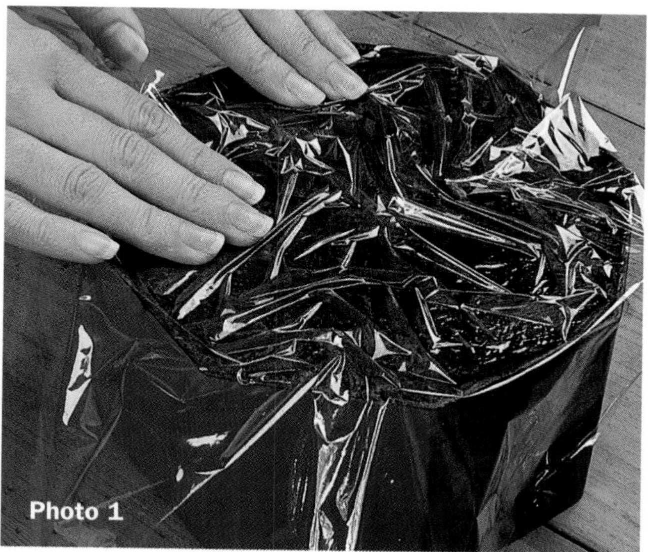
Photo 1

Photo 2

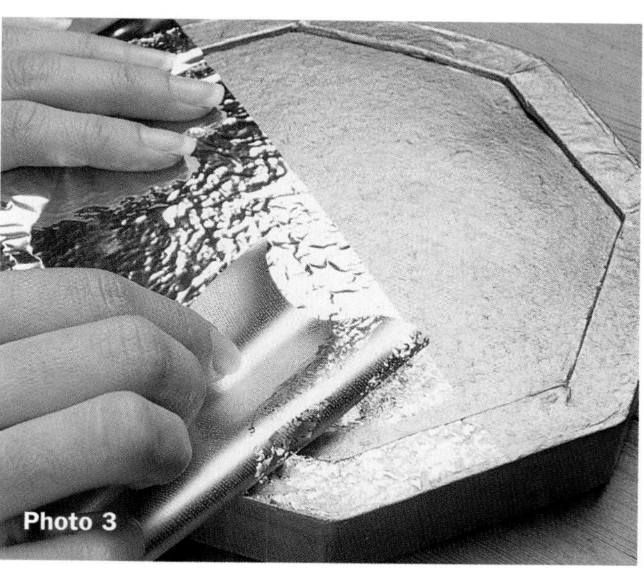
Photo 3

1. Paint box with base coat of green acrylic paint. Paint lid with base coat of gold acrylic paint. Let dry.

2. For leather effect on box, apply antiquing medium over green base coat, working on 1 section at a time and beginning with bottom of box. Lay piece of plastic wrap over wet antiquing medium. Wrinkle plastic by pressing with your fingertips **(Photo 1).** Peel off plastic wrap. As plastic is removed, antiquing medium will remain on plastic in areas, and green base coat will show through. Continue this process for entire box, using clean piece of plastic wrap for each section. Let dry.

3. For box lid, sponge foil bond onto lid over gold base coat **(Photo 2).** Let dry. As it dries, color of foil bond will change from milky white to clear. Press foil, shiny side up, onto bond. Carefully peel off foil **(Photo 3).**

4. For stud effect, dip end of paintbrush into gold paint and dot paint around outside of box. Let dry. To seal, spray box and lid with acrylic sealer.

Sunflower Napkin Rings

Look no further than the pantry for the supplies you'll need to make these soda-and-cornstarch blooms.

You will need (for 6 flowers):

flower and center patterns
tracing paper
posterboard or heavy paper
medium-sized saucepan
½ cup baking soda
¼ cup cornstarch
⅜ cup cold water
damp kitchen towel
cutting board
rolling pin
sharp, pointy knife
metal cookie sheet
waxed paper
fine-grade sandpaper
acrylic paints: dark green, yellow, red-orange
paintbrush
black dimensional paint
clear acrylic spray sealer
6 (2¾"-diameter) mini grapevine wreaths
hot-glue gun and glue sticks

1. For flower, trace flower pattern with pencil onto tracing paper and cut out. Transfer pattern onto posterboard or heavy paper and cut out. Repeat for flower center pattern.

2. In saucepan, mix baking soda, cornstarch, and water. Cook mixture over medium heat, stirring constantly until thick. (Texture should resemble that of mashed potatoes.) Remove from heat. Cover mixture with damp kitchen towel and let cool until it can be easily handled.

3. Lightly sprinkle cutting board with baking soda; place mixture on board. Using rolling pin, roll out mixture ⅛" to 3/16" thick.

4. Using flower pattern and knife, cut out 6 flowers from mixture. Carefully place flowers on waxed paper-lined cookie sheet. Cover flowers with damp kitchen towel to keep moist.

5. To shape flowers, use your forefinger and thumb to gently form rounded edges of flowers into soft points (see photo at left). Let dry overnight, turning flowers occasionally to ensure even drying and to prevent warping. (Climate may vary drying time.)

6. When completely dry, lightly sand rough edges. Using flower center pattern, trace center with pencil onto each flower.

7. Paint flower centers dark green. Paint flower petals and backs yellow. Let dry. To finish, lightly paint yellow details on centers and red-orange details on petals (see photo at left). Let dry. Using black dimensional paint, add dots to flower centers (see photo at left). Let dry. Spray flowers with acrylic sealer. Let dry.

8. To add rings, lay flowers facedown and hot-glue 1 mini wreath to each back. Let dry.

Soda-and-cornstarch dough is an inexpensive substitute for purchased roll-and-bake craft clay.

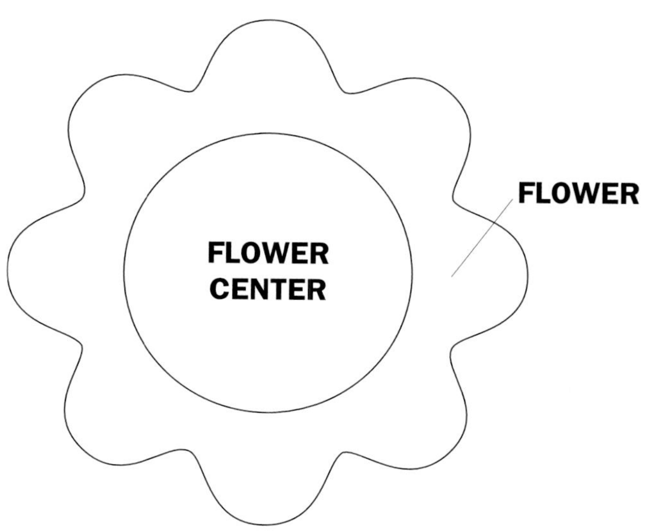

Pinecone Starters

For a quick warm-up, kindle your fire with wax-coated pinecones.

Add spice with a drop of cinnamon fragrance in the wax.

You will need (for 6 starters):

6 (4"-long) candlewicks
6 large pinecones
medium-sized saucepan
3 (1-pound) boxes paraffin
1 (3-pound) empty coffee can
2 (¾-ounce) packages cinnamon fragrance
2 (¾-ounce) packages wax dye
waxed paper

1. Tie 1 end of 1 wick to top of each pinecone. Set aside.

2. Fill saucepan with several inches of water. Place 1½ pounds of paraffin in coffee can. Set can in saucepan; melt paraffin over medium heat. Stir in 1 package of fragrance and 1 package of dye. Remove pan from heat and let wax slightly cool.

3. Dip 1 pinecone several times into liquid paraffin. Place on waxed paper to cool. Three pinecones will use 1½ pounds of paraffin. Repeat steps 2 and 3 with remaining pinecones.

4. To use, light wick and carefully place starter in center of logs in fireplace.

Medium- to large-sized pinecones can be found outdoors any time of year, but they're most abundant in the fall.

tip

For a housewarming present, surprise a friend or a neighbor with a batch of pinecone starters. Package the starters in a fabric sack accented with raffia or twine. Or pile them in a basket tied with ribbon. Include a card with instructions for using the starters (see Step 4).

Fabric Envelopes

Fuse scraps together to enclose recipes, photographs, and other small treasures.

For the envelope lining, we used a scrap of fabric in colors to coordinate with the outer fabric.

You will need (for each):

desired paper envelope
fusible web
desired fabric scraps
rotary cutter (optional)
iron
Velcro™ tabs (optional)

1. Carefully unfold paper envelope and lay it flat. Trace envelope shape onto paper backing of fusible web.

2. Following manufacturer's directions, fuse web to wrong side of outer envelope fabric. Cut out envelope shape. (For smooth and even edges, use rotary cutter.)

3. Remove paper backing from fusible web and fuse fabric to wrong side of envelope lining fabric. Cut out envelope shape.

4. Using intact envelope as guide, fold side flaps toward center. Then fold bottom flap up. Secure bottom flap to side flaps with strips of fusible web.

5. Using iron or fingertips, press side and bottom edges of envelope. Fold down top flap and press edge. If desired, use small strips of fusible web or Velcro tabs to keep envelope closed.

Unfold the paper envelope and lay it flat. Trace the envelope shape onto the paper backing of the fusible web. Fuse the web onto the outer envelope fabric and cut out the shape.

Sheer Sachets

Save a rosy scent inside squares of organza.

You will need (for 8 sachets in same color):

⅓ yard 45"-wide organza or organdy (We used silk organdy.)
needle and thread to match fabric
purchased rose petal potpourri
#20 chenille needle
4-mm silk ribbon

Note: Finished size of each sachet is 4" square.

1. For each sachet, cut 2 (5") squares. With right sides facing and raw edges aligned, use needle and thread to handstitch pieces together on 3 sides, using ½" seam allowance. Turn sachet to right side. Finger-press creases along sewn edges and corners.

2. Turn raw edges of sachet to inside ½"; finger-press. Using needle and thread, make large running stitches to baste a pocket ½" inside stitched sides of sachet. Fill pocket with potpourri. Baste pocket closed ½" from folded edges of sachet. To finish off fourth side of sachet, slipstitch folded edges together.

3. Using chenille needle and silk ribbon and referring to stitching diagrams, embroider sachet between basting stitches and outer edges. To thread needle, pierce ribbon ¼" from end; gently pull opposite ribbon end to secure **(Threading Needle).** Remove basting.

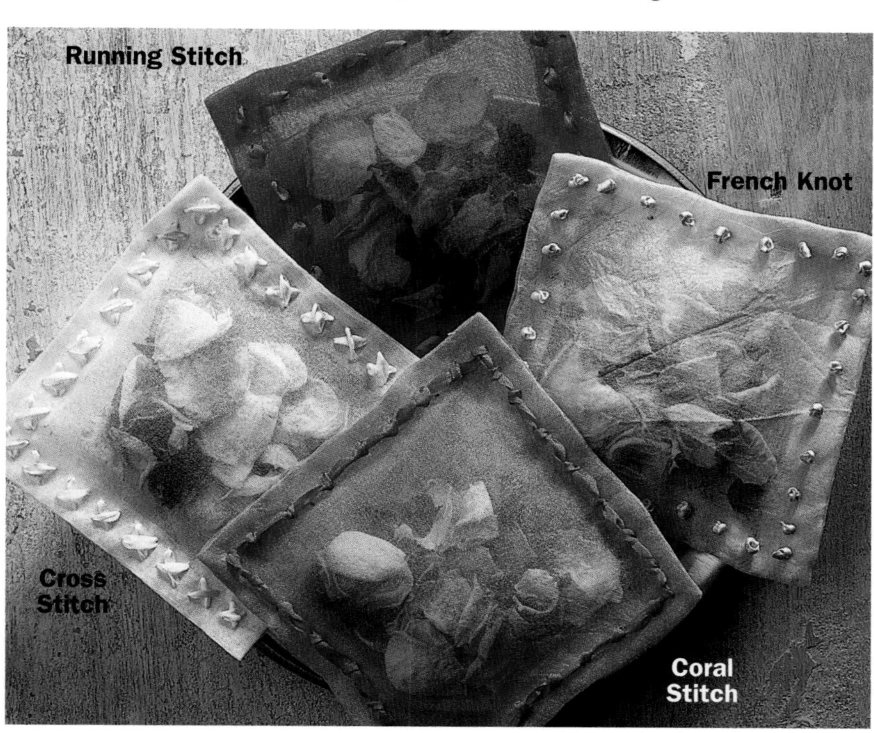

Threading Needle

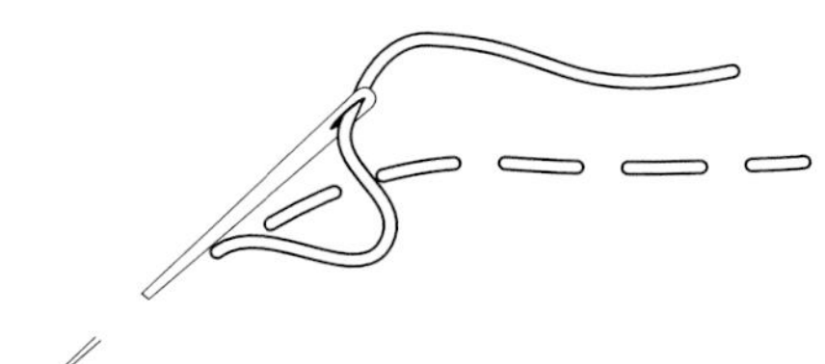

Running Stitch

Cross Stitch

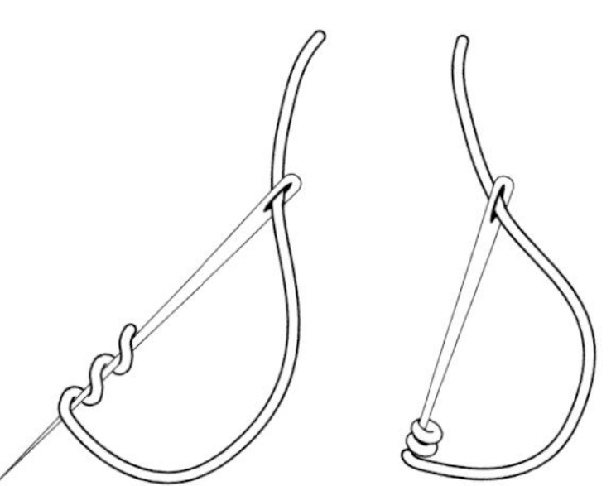

French Knot

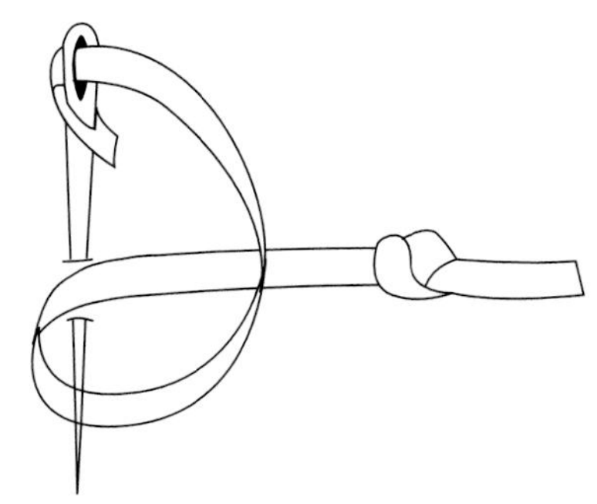

Coral Stitch

Plate Pizzazz

Hand-painted glass dishes make a tasty table setting.

The enamel paint we used is dishwasher safe.

You will need:

clear glass plates
white chargers
newspaper
tracing paper
masking tape
Liquitex® Glossies™ acrylic enamel glass paints: black, yellow, red, purple, blue, green
small paintbrush

1. Clean and dry plates before painting. Cover work surface with newspaper. Trace desired pattern onto tracing paper.

2. For each plate, referring to photo, position desired pattern facedown on top of plate. Secure pattern with small piece of tape. Turn plate over on work surface so that bottom of plate is faceup.

3. Following pattern outline and using paintbrush, paint design onto bottom of plate with black paint. Let dry. Turn plate over and remove pattern. Referring to Step 2 and photo, reposition pattern on plate and paint. To reposition and repeat wave pattern, align wavy line pattern with painted wavy line; then paint to continue wavy line. Repeat steps 2 and 3 until all desired designs are painted onto plate.

4. Referring to photo and using paintbrush, paint over and inside designs with desired color paint. Let dry. Follow paint manufacturer's directions for curing paint to make dishwasher safe.

5. For each charger, using paintbrush and black paint, paint small ½"-long dashes around outside edge (see photo). Let dry.

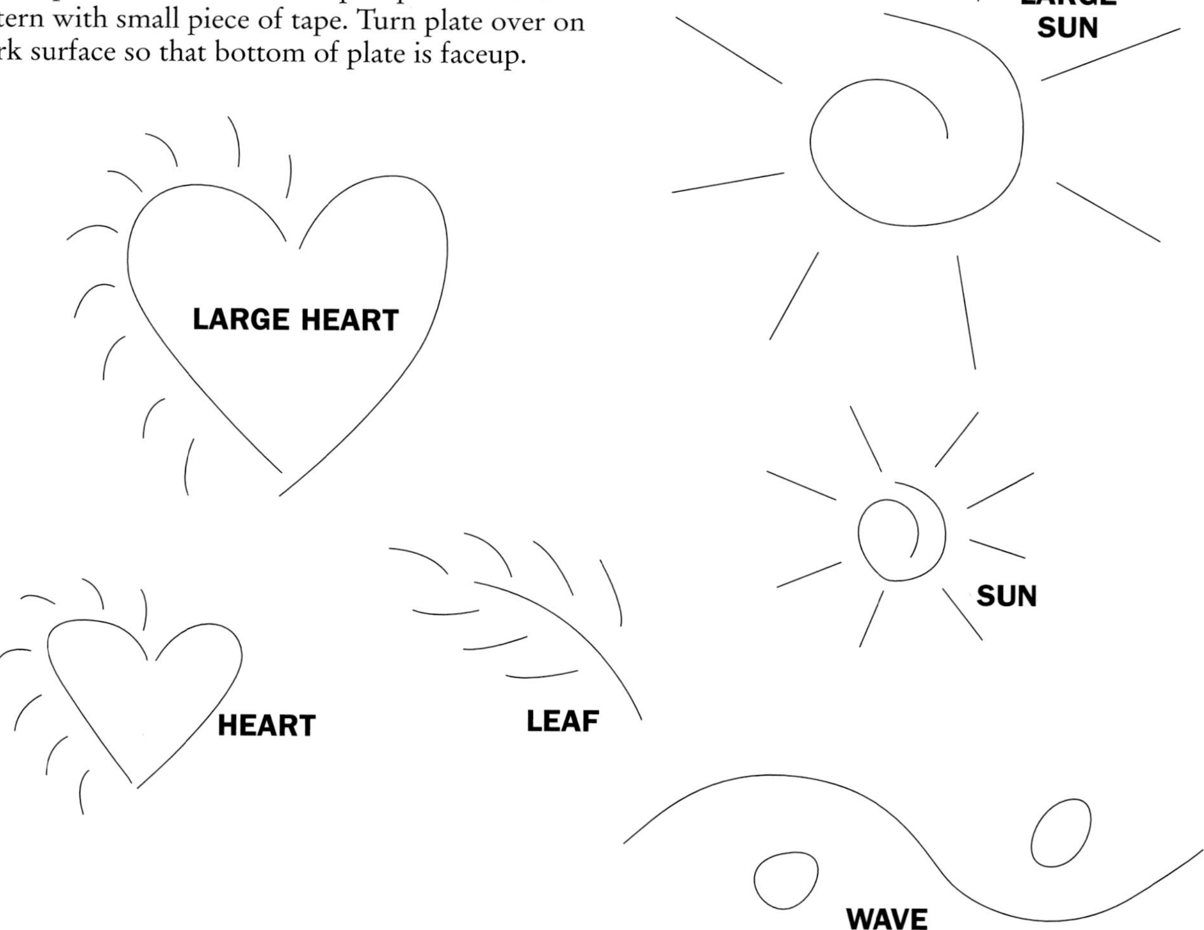

Styles for Tiles

Assorted tiles become a handsome set of household helpers.

Trivets

Bookends

Planter

Boxes

Purchase tile remnants from home improvement stores. Some stores will even cut the tiles for you.

You will need:

For each:

heavy food cans
masking tape
clear silicone glue

For planter:

5 (8") square tiles
4 (4") square tiles
4 (3") square tiles

For boxes:

6 (4") square tiles for large box
4 (2") square tiles for large box
1 (2") square tile cut in half for large box handle
6 (3") square tiles for small box
5 (1") square tiles for small box
premixed latex tile grout
small putty knife
5 marbles for small box

For bookends:

1 (6" x 8") tile cut in half widthwise for large bookends
1 (3" x 8") bullnose tile cut in half widthwise for large bookends
2 (3") square tiles each for large and small bookends
2 (2") square tiles each for large and small bookends
2 (4") square single bullnose tiles for small bookends
1 (4") square bullnose tile cut in half for small bookends
felt to match tiles

For trivets:

1 (8") square tile for large trivet
1 (4") square tile for small trivet
4 (2"-diameter) wooden drawer pulls for large trivet
4 (1"-diameter) wooden drawer pulls for small trivet

Note: Use heavy food cans to hold tiles in place as you glue them together. Use masking tape to temporarily secure decorative tiles while glue dries.

Assembly Diagram

1. For **planter,** referring to **Assembly Diagram,** glue together 4 (8") tiles to form an open box. Let dry. Glue remaining 8" tile to planter bottom. Let dry. To reinforce corners of planter, apply glue along inside corners. Let dry. Referring to photo, glue 1 (4") tile and 1 (3") tile to center of each planter side. Let dry.

2. For each **box,** glue 1 tile to each side of 1 bottom tile, using 4" tiles for large box and 3" tiles for small box. Let dry. Using putty knife, spread grout along each corner on outside of box, pressing grout into crevices (see photo). Smooth and remove excess grout with putty knife. Let dry. For **large box,** glue 1 (2") tile to center of each box side. Let dry. For **small box,** glue 1 (1") tile and 1 marble to center of each box side (see photo). Let dry. For **large box lid,** with wrong sides together, glue halves of 2" tile together. Let dry. Referring to photo, glue halves to center of remaining 4" tile. Let dry. For **small box lid,** glue remaining 1" tile and marble to center of remaining 3" tile. Let dry.

3. For **bookends,** referring to photo, glue tiles together at 90° angle. For each **large bookend,** glue 1 half of 6" x 8" tile to 1 half of 3" x 8" tile. Let dry. Glue 1 (3") tile and 1 (2") tile to large tile (see photo). Let dry. For each **small bookend,** glue 1 (4") tile to 1 half of 4" tile. Let dry. Glue 1 (3") tile and 1 (2") tile to large tile (see photo). Let dry. Measure and cut felt to fit bottom and back of each bookend. Glue felt pieces in place on bookends. Let dry.

4. For each **trivet,** glue 1 drawer pull to each corner on bottom of trivet. Let dry.

Papier-mâché Bowls

These fabulous creations all started with a balloon and tissue paper.

You will need (for each):

balloon
small piece of wood
thumbtack
wallpaper paste
sponge brush
assorted colors tissue paper
assorted colors embroidery floss
clear acrylic spray sealer

1. For bowl mold, blow up balloon and knot opening to secure. Curve of balloon makes mold for bowl; top of balloon forms middle of bowl. To position balloon, tack balloon to piece of wood.

2. Referring to manufacturer's instructions, mix wallpaper paste. Tear tissue paper into 1" x 3" strips. Using sponge brush and paste, attach each strip as desired onto balloon, thoroughly saturating tissue with paste.

3. Attach and arrange strips for desired design on inside of bowl **(Photo 1).** Layer strips in 1 direction over design to form inside and shape of bowl. Then attach another layer of strips perpendicular to first layer **(Photo 2).** Let 2 layers dry for approximately 10 minutes. Continue adding layers in this manner for total of 5 to 6 layers.

4. For added texture and design on inside of bowl, use pieces of floss as desired. To form floss design, first attach 1 layer of tissue for base layer. (For floss color to show through tissue on inside of bowl, use light-colored tissue for base layer.) Arrange and attach floss on tissue base as desired. Referring to Step 3, continue covering floss with layers of tissue strips **(Photo 3).**

5. Let tissue dry overnight. When tissue is completely dry, untie balloon to deflate it. Peel balloon away from tissue bowl. Trim and even edges of bowl with scissors. To finish, spray entire bowl with acrylic sealer. Let dry.

Photo 1

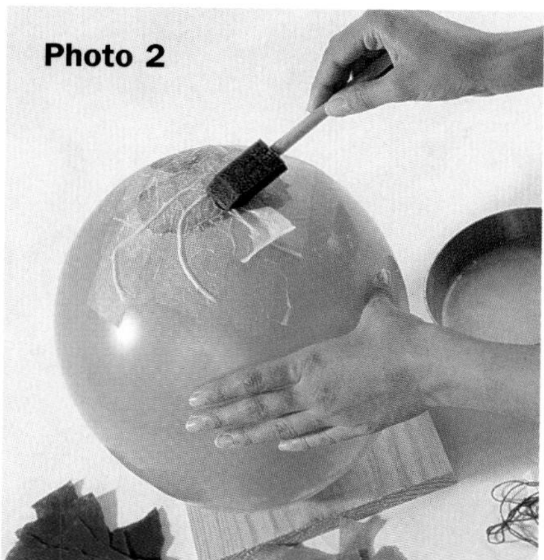
Photo 2

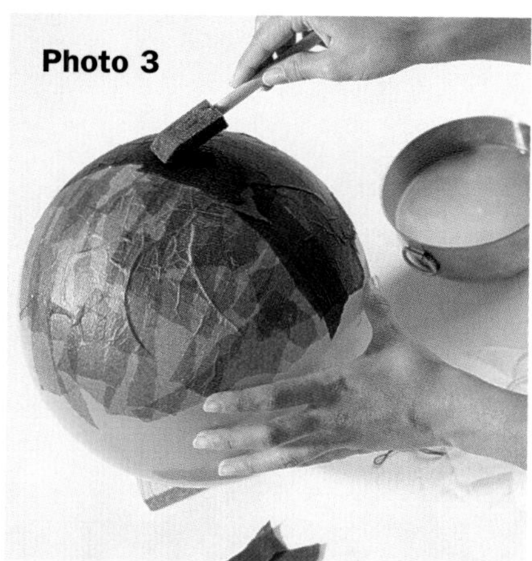
Photo 3

Christmas

Make your gifts and trimmings for a simpler, more satisfying holiday season. Add a dash of cheer to your table with our charming reindeer made from woodland finds. Hang tartan ribbon apples from your tree. Encircle your tree with a red felt skirt gladdened by a forest of firs and a galaxy of stars. Adorn your mantel with Christmas memories in the guise of a photo-pocket stocking rimmed in a simple blanket stitch.

page 116

page 102

page 110

page 98

Starry Night Tree Skirt

Glue happy holiday shapes right onto this no-sew skirt.

Get a head start on your tree skirt with a precut felt circle, available at many crafts stores.

You will need:

tracing paper
9" x 12" sheets felt: 4 each kelly green, apple green, chartreuse, and gold; 8 hunter green
dressmaker's chalk
1½ yards 54"-wide red felt or 54"-diameter precut red felt circle
pushpin
1 yard string
thick craft glue
1⅓ yards 1"-wide yellow ribbon

Note: Finished skirt is 54" in diameter.

1. Using tracing paper and dressmaker's chalk, transfer patterns to felt. From kelly green, apple green, and chartreuse, cut 15 trees each. From hunter green, cut 30 trees. From gold, cut 1 moon and 9 each of small star and large star.

2. To find center of 54" felt square, fold in half and then fold in half widthwise. Using pushpin, string, and pencil to make your own compass, mark inner and outer circles as indicated **(Cutting Diagram).** Cut through all layers along marked lines. If using precut circle, mark and cut out inner circle. Open skirt. Cut straight line from outer edge to inner circle for opening.

3. Referring to photo at left, glue trees in groups of 5 along edge of skirt. Glue stars and moon randomly to top of skirt. Let dry.

4. For ties, cut 4 (12") pieces of ribbon. On wrong side of skirt, glue 1 ribbon to each top edge of opening. Repeat with remaining ribbons at bottom edge of opening. Let dry. Tie ribbons together to close skirt.

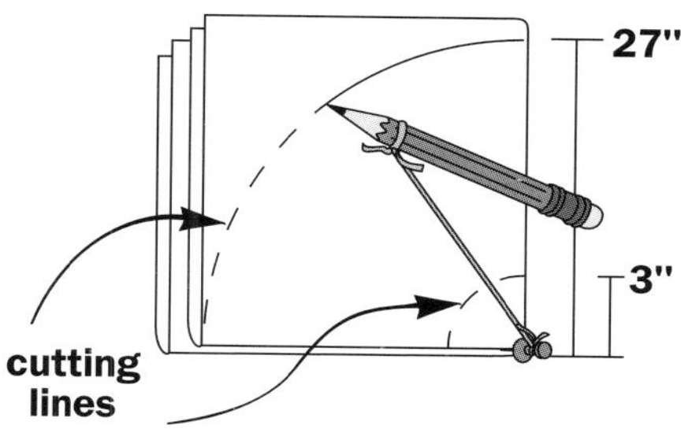

Cutting Diagram

Use the patterns to make felt ornaments. Using contrasting embroidery floss and a running stitch, stitch two shapes together. To make a hanger, take a stitch through the ornament top and knot the floss ends together.

MOON

TREE

STARS

Winter Wonder Pillow

Iron our folksy holiday scene onto a plain pillow and paint it with glee.

You will need:

5/8 yard medium-weight cream fabric (We used canvas.)
Winter Wonder iron-on transfer (See page 155.)
dressmaker's pencil
acrylic paints: medium blue, dark green, red, yellow, dark brown, terra-cotta, white
textile medium
small paintbrushes
black permanent fabric marker
2½ yards 1⅜"-wide red-and-black checked ribbon
liquid ravel preventer
hot-glue gun and glue sticks
pinking shears
4 (1 3/16") buttons
thread to match checked ribbon
green embroidery floss or pearl cotton

1. Cut 2 (19") squares from fabric. On right side of fabric, transfer iron-on pattern to center of 1 square. Measure and mark square 1½" outside design with dressmaker's pen. Using marked lines as placement guide, transfer iron-on holly border to fabric.

2. Following manufacturer's instructions, add a small amount of textile medium to paints to make them thinner and easier to work with. Referring to photo, paint design. Add white to dark brown to create color for rabbit. Let dry. Using permanent fabric marker, trace over black lines, covering any paint that might have spread. Let dry.

3. To mark flange, measure and lightly pencil square 2½" from outer edge of pillow front. With right sides facing and raw edges aligned, stitch pillow front and back together, using ¼" seam allowance. Leave 10" opening for turning along center of 1 side. Turn pillow right side out. Press seams on edge. Press seam allowance to inside along opening.

For flange, stitch along marked line, beginning at bottom edge, 2" from corner. Stitch around square, ending at bottom edge, 2" from opposite corner.

4. Cut 4 (18") lengths from ribbon. Apply liquid ravel preventer to cut ends. For each length, position along 1 end of pillow and trim to fit. Hot-glue each length to flange on pillow front, ¼" from edge.

5. Using pinking shears, cut 4 (4") lengths from remaining ribbon. Apply liquid ravel preventer to cut ends. Gather middle of each strip and tie with thread. Run green embroidery floss through holes of each button; tie floss ends together on back. Hot-glue 1 ribbon and 1 button to each pillow corner (see photos). Let dry.

6. Insert pillow form. Stitch pillow opening closed along marked line. Slipstitch flange opening closed.

To accent the corners of the pillow flange, thread a button with green embroidery floss and hot-glue it to a checked ribbon bow. Hot-glue the bow to the flange.

Ribbon-Wrapped Apples

Twist tartan plaids around a Styrofoam ball for these appealing ornaments.

You will need (for each):

1 (3"-diameter) Styrofoam ball
straight pins
3 yards ⅞"-wide plaid ribbon (See note below.)
½"-wide brown florist's tape
2 (2¼") velvet florist's leaves with wires
wire cutters

When making a set of ornaments, select ribbons in complementary colors. For the stem, wrap the florist's leaves and the ribbon tails with florist's tape.

Note: You can use ½"- to 1½"-wide ribbon. Yardage requirements will be greater for narrower ribbon and less for wider ribbon.

1. Mark top and bottom of ball with pins. Make tight 180° clockwise twist in ribbon, 1½" from 1 end. Pin twist to top of ball, leaving 2" ribbon tail free. Wrap ribbon to bottom of ball and then make 180° clockwise twist. Pin twist to bottom of ball **(Diagram 1).**

Diagram 1

2. Wrap ribbon to top of ball. Twist ribbon and pin to complete first round **(Diagram 2).**

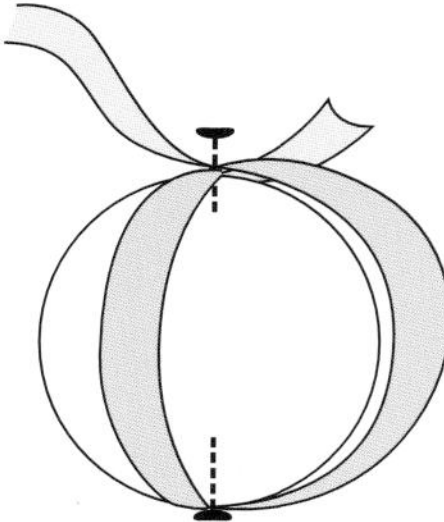

Diagram 2

3. Continue to wrap and twist ribbon to cover ball, overlapping edges of ribbon ⅛" **(Diagram 3).** To reduce bulk at top and bottom of ball, use pins only as needed after first round. At end, twist ribbon and pin, leaving 2" ribbon tail. Trim both tails at 45° angle.

Diagram 3

4. To make stem, holding both tails as 1, tightly wrap florist's tape twice around tails, starting at top of ball. (Florist's tape must be stretched in order to be sticky.) Referring to photo at left, place leaves on top of ball and wrap tape around wire and tails. Form a 2" stem, trimming excess wire with wire cutters. For hanger, form hook at end of stem.

Holiday Happies

For a handy gift, attach bells, buttons, or brads to make plain mittens merry.

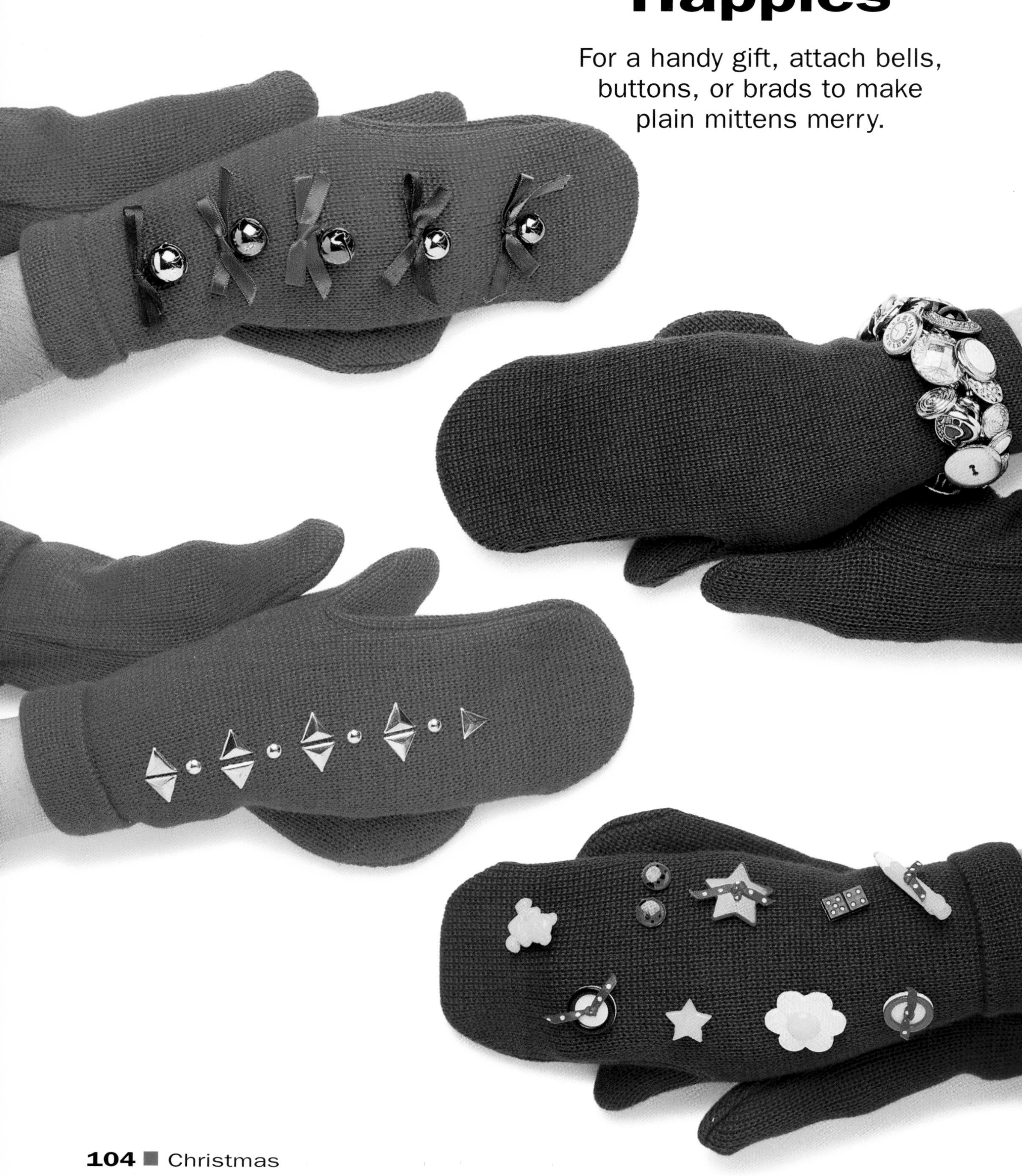

You will need:

Novelty Mittens
purchased mittens
assorted buttons: novelty shank-style, 2-hole
needle and thread to match mittens
large-eyed needle (capable of fitting through button holes)
1/16"- or 1/8"-wide ribbon
liquid ravel preventer

Brad Mittens
purchased mittens
brads in assorted styles
fabric glue

Bracelet Mittens
purchased mittens
wide-link chain (See Step 1 for yardage.)
wire cutters
pliers
needle and thread to match mittens
assorted buttons: shank-style, 2-hole

Jingle Mittens
purchased mittens
1/4"-wide ribbon in assorted colors to complement jingle bells
10 miniature jingle bells in assorted colors
liquid ravel preventer
needle and thread to match mittens

Novelty Mittens

1. Position buttons as desired on mittens to determine spacing. Stitch shank-style buttons in place, leaving space for remaining buttons.

2. To attach each 2-hole button, thread large-eyed needle with 1/16"- or 1/8"-wide ribbon. Attach button to mitten with ribbon, leaving ribbon tails on top. Remove needle and knot ribbon tails to secure. Trim ends, leaving 1/2" tails. Apply liquid ravel preventer to cut ends of ribbon.

Brad Mittens

Arrange brads on top of mittens. Following manufacturer's instructions, attach brads, adding drop of fabric glue under each to secure.

Bracelet Mittens

1. Measure circumference of 1 mitten cuff. Use wire cutters to cut two lengths of chain to this measurement. (We used an old necklace.) Using pliers, pry open link at 1 end of each length of chain. To form each bracelet, attach link to other end of chain and crimp tightly to close.

2. Whipstitch 1 bracelet to each mitten cuff, approximately 1" from top.

3. Stitch buttons to bracelet links, passing needle through mitten cuff occasionally to secure.

Jingle Mittens

1. Cut ribbons into 8" lengths. Tie each length in bow on shank of 1 bell. Apply liquid ravel preventer to cut ends of ribbons.

2. Tack 5 bells to top of each mitten, stitching through shanks and bows.

Coppery Christmas Ornaments

Shape flexible sheets of craft metal into twinkling treasures.

Craft metal comes in a variety of thicknesses. We used paper-thin 36-gauge metal, which can be cut with scissors.

You will need (for each):

tracing paper
1 (6" x 10") piece 36-gauge copper craft metal
dull pointed tool for embossing (dry ball-point pen or orange stick)
newspaper stack (for padded surface)
ruler
sharp pointed tool for punching (ice pick or punching awl)
epoxy resin
silk cording
cloth gloves (optional)
masking tape (optional)

Note: Craft metal has sharp edges. When working with it, wear gloves or cover metal edges with masking tape.

1. For each design, trace pattern with pencil onto tracing paper. Transfer pattern twice onto metal with embossing tool. Using scissors, cut out design along traced lines.

2. For each **tree,** emboss details. Place metal design (dull side up) on flat, padded surface. Place pattern on top of metal, aligning edges. Using ruler to steady embossing tool and working in 1 direction, trace detail lines, pressing gently to emboss metal. Use punching tool to make holes where indicated on pattern.

3. For each **star,** crimp points. Beginning at base of each point and working toward tip, fold metal accordion-style **(Crimping Diagram).**

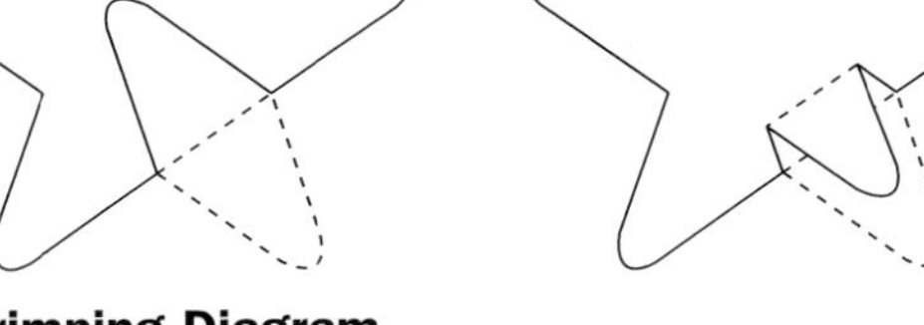

Crimping Diagram

4. To fit pieces together, make 2¼"-long vertical cut on each, starting at top on 1 piece and starting at bottom on remaining piece. With pieces at right angles, interlock pieces along cut lines to form 3-dimensional shape (see photo). Glue along cut lines with epoxy resin to secure.

5. For hanger, use punching tool to make small hole in top of 1 piece. Thread cording through hole and knot ends together.

- Craft metal is available in copper, brass, silver (aluminum), blue, and red. Use metal in different colors as desired to achieve the look you want.
- To antique the shiny finish of craft metal, wipe the metal with vinegar.

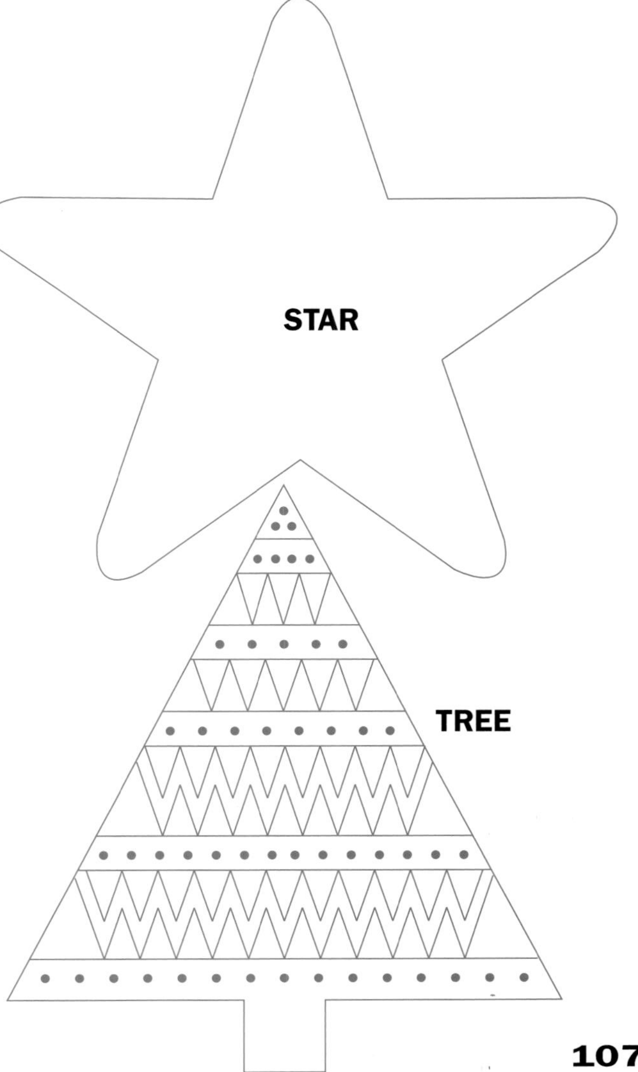

Naturally Festive Frames

Make flat, unfinished frames spectacular with a little glue and such natural objects as nuts, twigs, and seashells.

Twig Frame

A practical gift, these frames can display snapshots once the holidays are over.

You will need:

For each:
1 purchased frame with 1½"-wide flat sides
ruler
hot-glue gun and glue sticks
clear acrylic spray sealer

For Twig Frame:
4 dozen straight twigs with similar diameters

For Shell Frame:
assorted shells

For Twine Frame:
12 yards twine

Twig Frame

1. Measure width of frame sides. Cut twigs to match measurement. Referring to photo, arrange and glue twigs horizontally in corners of frame. Let dry.

2. Measure remaining spaces. Cut twigs to match measurements. Referring to photo, arrange and glue twigs vertically to fill in top, bottom, and sides of frame. Let dry.

3. To finish frame, spray with 2 coats of acrylic sealer, letting dry between each application.

Shell Frame

1. Measure width of frame sides. If possible, select shells with width to match. Glue these shells to frame. Let dry.

2. Glue smaller shells between larger shells to fill in. Overlap shells as necessary to cover frame (see photo below). Let dry.

3. To finish frame, spray frame with 2 coats of acrylic sealer, letting dry between each application.

Twine Frame

1. Cut 10" piece of twine. Coil twine into 1" circle, securing ends of coil with dots of glue. Glue coil to frame. Let dry. Repeat to cover frame with coils. Overlap coils as necessary to cover frame (see photo below). Let dry.

2. To cover outside edges of frame, wrap twine several times around edges, gluing as you wrap. When edges are covered, cut end of twine and secure to frame edge with glue.

3. To finish frame, spray frame with 2 coats of acrylic sealer, letting dry between each application.

Photo-Pocket Stocking

Christmas memories shine through a clear vinyl pocket.

The blanket stitches bordering this stocking are ¼" long and ¼" apart. Don't worry about slight variations—they'll only add charm.

You will need:

tracing paper
dressmaker's chalk
⅓ yard each polar fleece: red, green, white
6" square vinyl
straight pins
black embroidery floss
darning needle
tape
fabric glue
½ yard ⅝"-wide red grosgrain ribbon
needle and thread to match stocking
photograph to fit pocket

TOE

1. Using tracing paper and dressmaker's chalk, transfer patterns to fleece and vinyl (see photo). For full-size stocking, extend pattern 5".

2. From red fleece, cut 2 stocking pieces. From green fleece, cut 1 heel, 1 toe, and 4 (1¾") squares for cuff. From white fleece, cut 1 pocket and 2 (3½" x 7") cuff pieces. From vinyl, cut 1 pocket.

3. Pin toe and heel in place on stocking front. Using embroidery floss and darning needle, blanket-stitch toe and heel along inside edges **(Blanket-stitch Diagram).**

4. Pin white fleece pocket to center of stocking front. Place vinyl pocket piece on fleece pocket and tape to secure. Do not pin vinyl. Blanket-stitch through both layers to attach fleece and vinyl pocket pieces to stocking front (see photo).

5. With wrong sides together and edges aligned, pin stocking front to stocking back. Blanket-stitch around edges of stocking, including outside edges of toe and heel on stocking front.

6. Referring to photo, arrange 4 green squares on 1 cuff piece. Glue squares in place, spreading glue only on inside edges that will not be blanket-stitched. Let dry.

7. Blanket-stitch appliquéd cuff piece to stocking front along top edge. Repeat to attach remaining cuff piece to stocking back. Blanket-stitch front and back cuff pieces together along sides. Blanket-stitch front and back cuff pieces along bottom edge.

8. For hanger, fold ribbon length in half. Using needle and thread, stitch ribbon ends to inside right corner of stocking back. To finish, slip desired photo inside vinyl pocket.

STOCKING

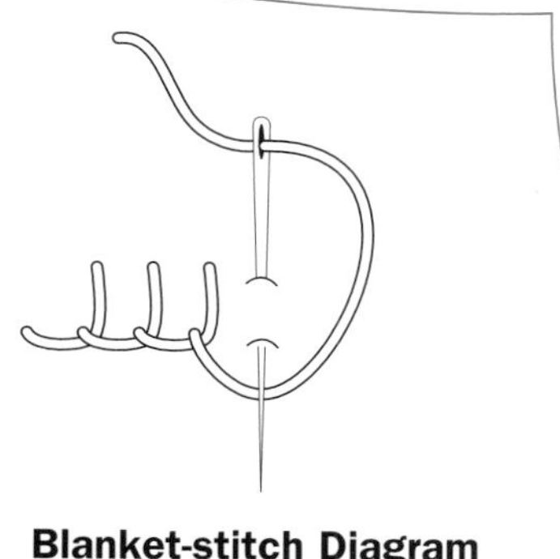

Blanket-stitch Diagram

POCKET

HEEL

Christmas Candy Cans
Color cans from your cupboard for these crafty containers.
Paper Silhouette Cans
Plaid Can
Button Can

You will need:

For each:

empty and clean soup, vegetable, or coffee tin can
wood scrap
nail or ice pick to make hole in can
hammer
gray spray primer
acrylic paints: red, green, white
paintbrushes
wire core paper twist for handle
wire cutters
jingle bells (optional)

For button can:

novelty Christmas buttons
low-temperature hot-glue gun and glue sticks

For paper silhouette can:

heavyweight craft paper
hole punch or decorative paper punch
craft glue

1. For each can, mark placement of holes on opposite sides of can for handle. Lay can on its side on top of wood scrap. Using hammer and nail or ice pick, punch holes at marks.

2. To prepare can for painting, spray can with primer. Let dry. Paint can with desired base color. Let dry.

3. To attach handle, thread wire through holes in can. Secure wire by wrapping wire ends around handle. To add jingle bells to handle, slip bells onto wire before threading wire through holes in can.

4. For **button can,** hot-glue novelty buttons onto can as desired (see photo at left). Let dry. For **plaid can,** referring to photo, paint horizontal stripes in ridges of can. Let dry. Paint vertical stripes between horizontal stripes. Let dry.

5. For **paper silhouette can,** transfer star or tree pattern to wrong side of paper as desired and cut out shapes. Using paper punch, cut out dots or stars from paper scraps. Using craft glue, glue paper shapes to can (see photo at left). Let dry.

Decorate the cans with acrylic paints and add a wire handle. To remove the labels from your cans, soak the cans in warm, soapy water for approximately 1 hour. Then carefully peel off the labels with a razor blade.

Holiday Door Swag

Ornaments dance on a length of raffia for a fun alternative to a wreath.

You will need:

roll of green raffia
1 yard twine
3 yards red wire-edged paper ribbon
florist's wire
assorted ornaments
large jingle bell
low-temperature hot-glue gun with glue sticks

1. Gather approximately 50 (54"-long) strands of raffia. Align ends of raffia as much as possible.

2. Fold gathered strands under 12" from 1 end, forming loop. Using 12"-long piece of twine, wrap and bind raffia strands together 6" from loop. Tie twine in knot.

3. For bow, fold ribbon under to form 4" loop at 1 end of ribbon **(Photo 1).** In same manner, fold ribbon under to form 7 more loops, pinching ends of loops together for center of bow **(Photo 2).**

4. Using florist's wire, tie loops together at center, twisting wire to secure **(Photo 3).** Leave wire ends loose at back of bow. Referring to photo on front of card, shape loops of bow. If needed, trim ribbon ends.

5. To attach bow to raffia swag, wrap wire ends on bow around twine binding, twisting wire to secure (see photo at left).

6. Hot-glue ornaments and jingle bell to front of swag as desired (see photo at left). Let dry. For hanger, loop remaining twine through raffia loop at top of swag. Knot twine ends together.

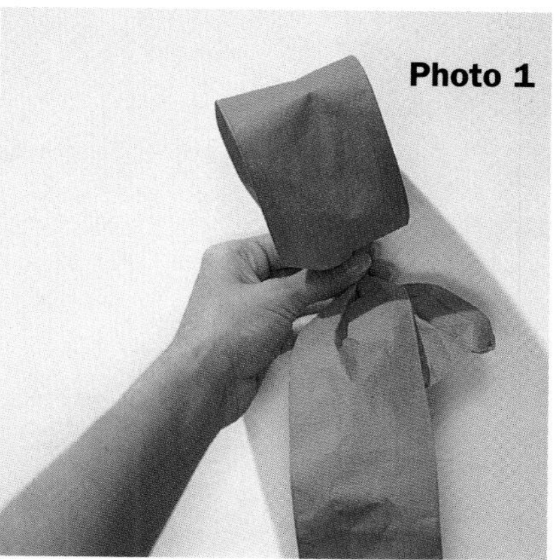

Photo 1

Photo 2

Photo 3

Santa's Reindeer

Woodland finds and fleecy red scarves wrap up this winsome trio.

For another adorable accent, tie a small jingle bell around each reindeer's neck instead of the fleece scarf.

You will need (for each):

assorted pinecones
assorted twigs
acorn top for nose
garden cutters
low-temperature hot-glue gun with glue sticks
1½" x 12" strip red polar fleece

1. For reindeer body, use 2 medium-sized pinecones. For reindeer head, cut top half off 1 pinecone, using garden cutters. Discard top. Hot-glue side of pinecone half to side of whole pinecone, aligning bottoms (see photos). Let dry.

2. For legs, referring to photos, hot-glue 2 twigs each to front and back of reindeer body. To attach each twig, apply hot-glue to 1 end of twig. Then insert glue-covered end of twig between pinecone scales, pushing until twig touches core of pinecone. Hold twig in place for a few seconds and let dry. When all twig legs are attached, use cutters to trim legs to even lengths until reindeer balances. You may have to trim legs with an angled cut to balance reindeer (see photos).

3. For antlers, use 2 twigs with small branches. Referring to Step 2, hot-glue twigs to top of reindeer head (see photos). Let dry.

4. Referring to photos, for nose, hot-glue acorn top to center of reindeer face. For tail, hot-glue 1 tiny pinecone to back end of reindeer body. To accent reindeer body, hot-glue several tiny pinecones behind head and underneath reindeer around legs. (Tiny pinecones simulate longer fur on reindeer.) Let dry.

5. For scarf, referring to photo below, cut fringe on each each end of fleece strip. Tie scarf around neck of reindeer.

Trimmed Treasures

Make plain glass ornaments magical by embellishing them with ribbon and cording.

Gold Rope and Tassel

Silver Swirl

Gold Rope and Swirl

You will need:

For each:

glass ornament (We used a 5" ornament.)
low-temperature glue gun and glue sticks
seam sealant

For silver swirl:

1½ yards 1/16"-diameter silver metallic cording

For gold rope and swirl:

1½ yards ¼"-diameter red-and-gold cording
1½ yards 1/16"-diameter gold metallic cording

For gold rope and tasssel:

¾ yard ⅛"-diameter gold-and-purple cording
1¾ yards 1/16"-diameter gold cording
1 (2") gold tassel

1. For **silver swirl ornament,** cut cording into 3 (18") lengths. Seal ends with sealant. Beginning at 1 end of cording, roll a 9" swirl and glue in center of ornament. Roll remaining end in opposite direction; glue in place, leaving ½" between coiled cord. Repeat around ornament.

2. For **gold rope and swirl ornament,** seal ends of red-and-gold cording with sealant. Glue 1 end to center back of ornament. Make 2 S shapes around ornament with cording, gluing in place as necessary. Repeat with remaining cording on opposite side. Cut metallic cord into 4 (7⅕") lengths. Seal ends with sealant to prevent fraying. Coil each length tightly and glue 1 in center of each half of S (see photo).

3. For **gold rope and tassel ornament,** cut 4 (6") lengths of each cording. Seal ends with sealant. Beginning at top of ornament, glue ends of lengths to ornament, alternating colors and leaving 1¼" distance between each at widest points. Glue top of tassel to bottom center of ornament. Cut 2 (18") lengths of 1/16" cording. Starting at center top point of ornament, coil 1 (18") length, gluing as necessary. Repeat for bottom of ornament, wrapping cording around tassel.

Super Quick

These projects are the answer when time is of the essence. Create charming candles in an instant by pouring wax crystals into teacups. Plain dishtowels bloom into cheery accessories with iron-on transfers and a bit of fabric paint. Transform a baking sheet into a regal server with a crown and diamond design. For fast crafting fun, whip up bookmark critters out of paper clips, pom poms, and wiggle eyes.

page 128
page 126
page 122
page 140

Bookmark Critters

You can make a menagerie of these place-holding creatures in an afternoon.

Experiment and give each of these critters a personality.

You will need:

cardboard scrap covered with aluminum foil
vegetable oil spray
low-temperature glue gun
colored glue sticks
regular and jumbo vinyl-coated paper clips in variety of colors
toothpicks
assorted feathers
faceted beads: 6-mm orange, gold, yellow, blue, green, and turquoise; 4-mm clear
7-mm movable eyes
5-mm pom-poms
chenille stems

Note: Before making a base from glue, arrange extra materials as you want them to appear on finished project. To avoid burning your fingers, use toothpicks to position all materials in glue.

1. For nonstick work surface, spray small area of foil with oil. To make base for 1 critter, form thick, quarter-sized circle of glue on oiled surface. Press tip of jumbo paper clip into glue to secure, making sure end that clips onto page stays out of glue.

2. Working quickly while glue is still wet and referring to steps below, press extra materials in place.

3. For **fish,** position feathers in glue to form tail and fin. Add another layer of glue to base. Position colored faceted beads and eye (see photo at left). To shape mouth, touch tip of glue gun against edge of glue circle. Glue will melt, forming semicircular mouth (see photo at left). Let dry.

4. For **bug or spider,** add small circle of glue for head. Unwind regular-sized paper clips to use for legs and antennae. Wrap straightened clips around pencil to curl. Position legs and antennae in glue. Add another layer of glue to base and head. Position pom-poms, clear faced beads, and eyes (see photos). Let dry.

5. For **bird**, add small circle of glue for head. Position feathers in glue. Add another layer of glue to base and head. Position pom-poms, chenille stems, and eyes (see photo at left). Add third layer of glue to base for stomach. Let dry.

tip

To change hot-glue colors, run a clear glue stick through the glue gun to clear out the excess color. Sometimes you get interesting swirls of color in this process, so don't let these go to waste.

Dimensional Photo Magnets

For twice the fun, glue photo cutouts to foam core to make 3-D pictures.

Completed Magnet

You will need:

double prints of desired photograph with matte finish (Matte finish allows dimensional paints to stand out from photograph.)
self-adhesive magnetic sheet
artist's adhesive spray
3/8"-thick foam-core board
tracing paper
dimensional paints in desired colors
craft knife
glue stick

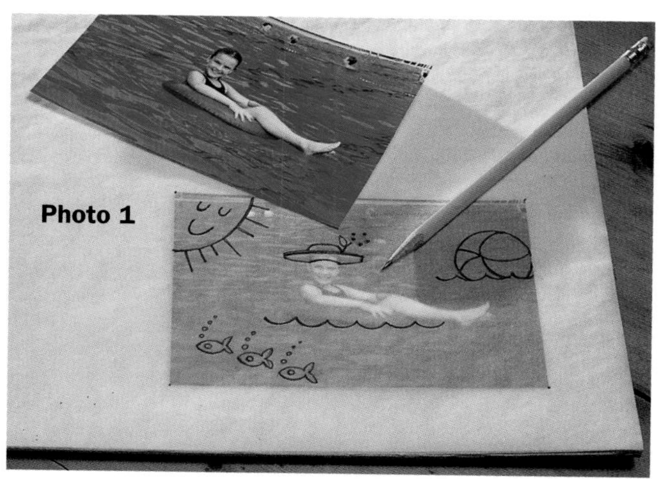

Photo 1

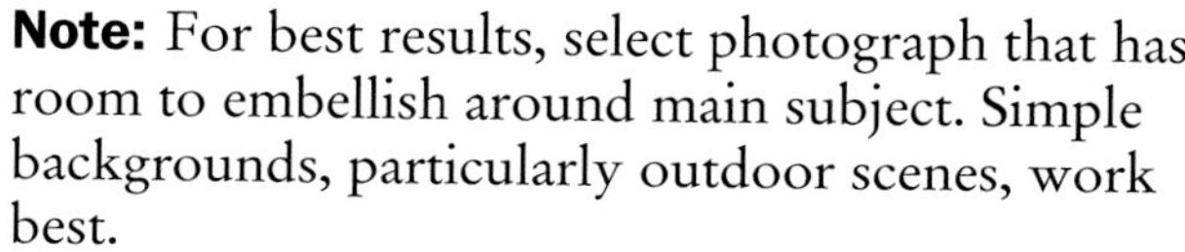

Note: For best results, select photograph that has room to embellish around main subject. Simple backgrounds, particularly outdoor scenes, work best.

Photo 2

1. Remove adhesive backing from magnetic sheet. Press to back of 1 photograph. Trim magnetic sheet to same size as photograph. Using adhesive spray, glue foam core to back of remaining photograph.

2. Place tracing paper over 1 photograph. Experiment with ways to embellish photograph by drawing on tracing paper **(Photo 1).** Try balloons, animals, ice-cream cones, big hats—whatever you think will best enhance photograph.

3. Referring to tracing paper sketch, embellish photographs as desired, using dimensional paints. To give finished project more depth, add paint details to both photographs **(Photo 2).** Let dry.

Photo 3

4. Using craft knife, cut out desired subject from foam-core photograph. Using glue stick, glue cutout directly over matching image on other photograph **(Photo 3).**

For a trip momento or a clever greeting card, glue your finished photograph to heavy cardstock instead of a magnetic sheet.

Teacup Candles

Wax crystals are the speedy secret behind these perky little party lights.

You will need (for each):

desired teacup and saucer
Candle Magic® wax crystals
Candle Magic® precoated wick
ribbon (optional)

Note: When using candle outdoors, do not tie ribbon on teacup; wind could blow ribbon into candle flame.

1. Pour wax crystals into teacup, filling to within ½" of brim **(Photo 1).** Smooth surface of wax crystals with fingertips or flat object like bottom of glass.

2. Push wick into center of wax crystals until end of wick touches teacup bottom. Trim top of wick to within ½" of wax crystals **(Photo 2).**

3. To seal surface of candle, place hot iron (on medium setting) 4" above wax crystals for approximately 3 minutes. Heat from iron will melt top layer of wax crystals, preventing wax crystals from spilling from teacup.

4. Light wick. Wax crystals will melt around base of flame **(Photo 3).**

tip

These pretty candles are practical for summer outdoor entertaining: just add citronella oil to keep bugs at bay. To add citronella or other essential oil to your wax crystal candles, pour 12 ounces of wax crystals into a zip-top plastic bag with ¼ ounce of oil. Close bag and shake, mixing wax crystals and oil.

Photo 1

Photo 2

Photo 3

Pretty Painted Dish Towels

Here's a remedy for kitchen blahs: transfer cheer to ordinary dish towels with these blooming iron-ons and paint.

Make matching kitchen accessories by adding these designs to place mats, napkins, and a tablecloth.

You will need (for each):

cotton dish towel
iron-on transfers (See page 157.)
scrap of fabric or thick paper
straight pins
cardboard covered with waxed paper
fabric paints in assorted colors
stiff-bristle paintbrush
fine-tip permanent black marker

1. Before transferring design, wash, dry, and iron dish towel. Do not use fabric softener in washer or dryer. Cut out desired transfer from page 157, leaving as much excess paper around design as possible. Place scrap of paper or fabric under flattened towel in case transfer bleeds through.

2. Place transfer facedown on right side of towel where desired. Pin in place. Place hot, dry iron on transfer. Do not use steam. Hold iron down for 5 to 10 seconds. Do not slide iron because this might smear design. Continue until all designs are transferred.

3. To paint designs, pin flattened towel to cardboard, smoothing out any wrinkles. Following manufacturer's instructions, paint designs with fabric paint and brush (see photo). Let paint dry between colors and coats. Several coats may be needed. Using black marker, outline design details. Heat-set paint. Launder towel according to paint manufacturer's instructions.

tip

Your iron's temperature setting, the time the iron stays on the transfer, and the amount of pressure you use will affect the number of times the design can be transferred.

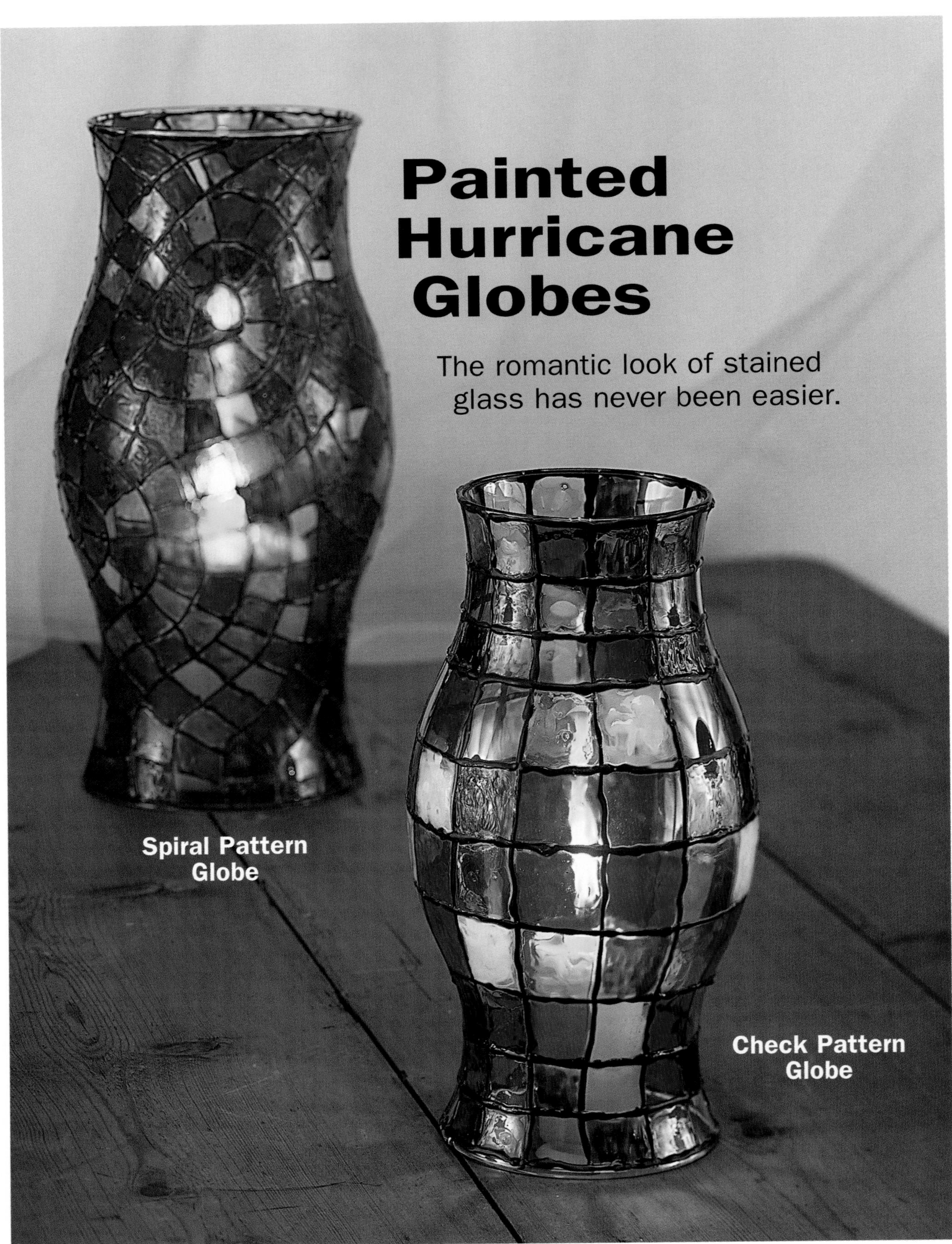

Painted Hurricane Globes

The romantic look of stained glass has never been easier.

Spiral Pattern Globe

Check Pattern Globe

For added interest, leave some areas on your lamp unpainted.

You will need:

hurricane lamp with glass globe
thin masking tape
liquid leading paint
transparent glass paints in assorted colors

1. Clean glass globe with soap and water. Dry thoroughly. For **check pattern globe,** use tape to mark horizontal lines around globe. Make lines gradually wider in middle portion of globe (see photo at left).

2. To hold globe while painting horizontal lines, insert your hand inside globe and turn globe with your fingers. Referring to photo and using tape as guide, paint horizontal lines with liquid leading. Let dry. Carefully remove tape. To paint vertical lines, while holding globe, paint lines with liquid leading. Make lines gradually wider in middle portion of globe (see photo at left). Let dry.

3. Referring to photo, fill in squares with 1 coat of glass paint. Let dry.

4. For **spiral pattern globe,** refer to photos at right. Holding globe in same manner as above and beginning at top of globe, paint S shape vertically on globe with liquid leading. Repeat on opposite side of globe. Paint spiral inside each curved part of each S shape, keeping lines evenly spaced. Fill in rest of globe by painting curved lines around spirals, keeping lines evenly spaced. Let dry. To make squares, connect curved lines with liquid leading, keeping squares of approximate size. Let dry. Referring to Step 3, fill in squares with glass paint.

For the Spiral Pattern Globe, left, begin by sketching the design with a pencil on a piece of paper. Then paint an S shape vertically on the globe. Paint a spiral inside each curved part of the S shape (see photo above).

Veggie Baskets

Turn everyday kitchen tools into great-looking storage for fruits and vegetables.

Screw a hook into your kitchen ceiling or cabinets to hang your veggie baskets.

You will need:

8"-diameter stainless steel bowl
12"-diameter stainless steel colander
drill with ¼" drill bit
10"-diameter round cooling rack
13 (1½"-long) S hooks
approximately 2½ yards small chain
wire cutters
hot-glue gun and glue sticks

1. For bowl and colander, drill a hole ¼" from rim at 4 equidistant points. Clip hooks onto bowl and colander at each drilled hole. Attach hooks to cooling rack to match those on colander.

2. Using wire cutters, cut chain into 4 (5½"-long) links and 8 (8"-long) links. Attach 5½" links to hooks of colander (see photos). Attach 8" links to hooks on cooling rack and bowl.

3. Referring to photograph at left, attach links from colander to cooling rack, from cooling rack to bowl, and from bowl to a single hook.

4. Dab small openings of hooks with glue to seal and prevent hooks from slipping out of holes. Let dry.

The S hooks secure the chains between the bowl, the cooling rack, and the colander.

tip

For a different look, you can substitute baskets for bowls.

Seashell Organizer

The beach-textured finish gets its grit from seashore sand.

Collect shells and empty snack containers for your organizer. You can purchase sand at garden shops.

Photo 1

You will need:

3 empty and clean cardboard snack containers
Instant Finishes™ Liquid Chalk: Linen #31353
sand
assorted seashells
raffia

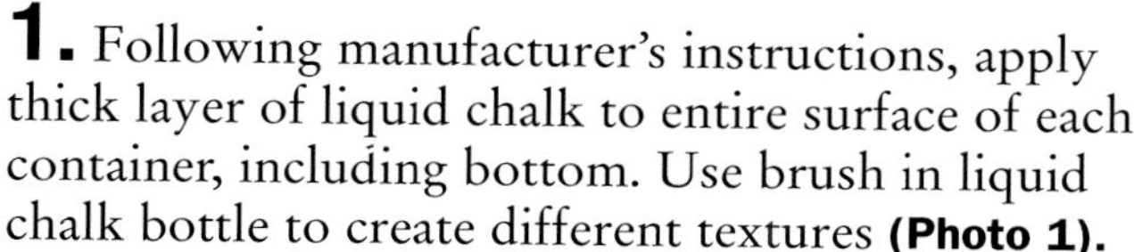

1. Following manufacturer's instructions, apply thick layer of liquid chalk to entire surface of each container, including bottom. Use brush in liquid chalk bottle to create different textures **(Photo 1).**

2. When liquid chalk has set but remains wet to touch, sprinkle sand as desired onto liquid chalk surface of each container. Then press shells as desired onto liquid chalk surface **(Photo 2).** Let dry. The sand and shells adhere to the liquid chalk as it dries on the container.

3. Referring to photo at left, stack containers in pyramid shape. Tie stack together with approximately 15 (48") raffia strands, tying bow at top.

Photo 2

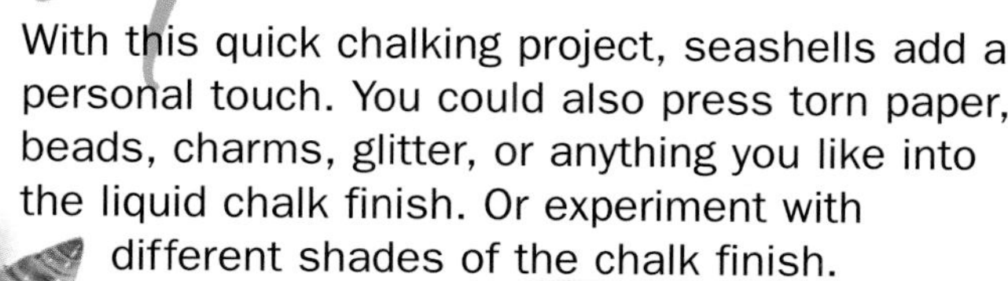

tip

With this quick chalking project, seashells add a personal touch. You could also press torn paper, beads, charms, glitter, or anything you like into the liquid chalk finish. Or experiment with different shades of the chalk finish.

Moss-Covered Planters

Sheet moss and bark quickly disguise plastic plant containers.

For a quick gift with a personal touch, cover a planter of purchased flowers with your own moss-and-bark design.

You will need (for each):

desired plant in plastic nursery pot
low-temperature glue gun and glue sticks
sheet moss
old metal spoon
bark (We used sweet gum tree bark.)
Spanish moss

1. Working on small area at a time, apply glue to pot. Cover glue-covered area with small piece of moss. Use back of spoon to press moss into glue. Repeat until pot is covered with moss. Let dry.

2. Glue strips of bark over moss around rim of pot. Experiment with bark to make different patterns in moss. For **crisscross design**, crisscross strips of bark and glue to sides of square moss-covered pot (see photo at left). Let dry.

3. To finish pot, tuck Spanish moss at base of plant.

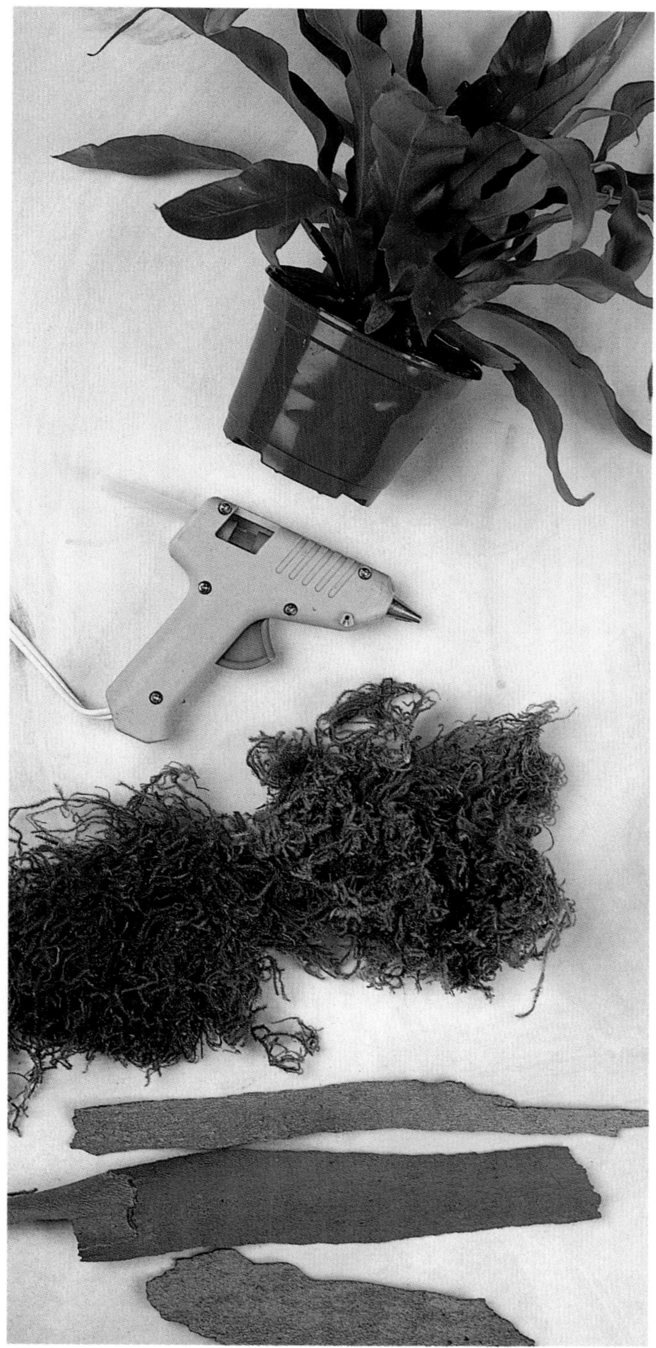

Using a low-temperature glue gun, carefully attach the moss and the bark to the plastic container of a purchased plant.

Speedy Pillow Slipcovers

Tie on scarves for fabulous pillows in minutes.

Square Pillows

Bolster Pillow

You will need (for each):

square or bolster pillow or form
desired square scarf (large enough to cover pillow)
ribbon to match scarf

1. Spread scarf flat on work surface. Place pillow in center of scarf with pillow sides parallel to corners of scarf.

2. To cover **square pillow,** pull 1 corner of scarf over pillow to opposite side of pillow **(Photo 1).** Then pull opposite corner of scarf over pillow, folding corner of scarf under at center **(Photo 2).** To finish, pull remaining corners of scarf over pillow and firmly tie them together in a knot at center **(Photo 3).** If desired, fold tie ends over knot and tuck them under knot (see photo at left).

3. For **bolster pillow,** beginning with pillow at 1 side of scarf, roll pillow to opposite side of scarf, wrapping scarf around pillow. To secure scarf around pillow, tie scarf with ribbon at each end of pillow (see photo at left).

tip

This idea for quickly covering pillows works with an unfinished square of lightweight fabric, too.

Photo 1

Photo 2

Photo 3

Tray Majestic

A serving tray fit for a king is simple to stencil.

Do not use cookie sheet with a nonstick surface because paint will not adhere.

You will need:

medium-sized metal cookie sheet
stencil pattern (See page 159.)
8 ½" x 11" sheet plastic template material
black marker
protective mat or cardboard
craft knife
masking tape
small round stencil brush
metallic gold acrylic paint
dimensional paints: iridescent chartreuse, iridescent magenta, navy blue, white
clear acrylic spray sealer (optional)

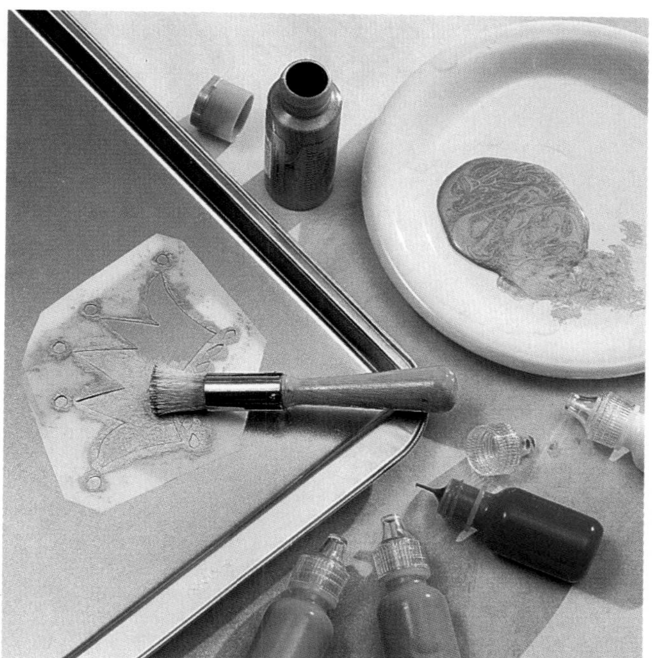

When you are stenciling a design, you need to use a thick coat of paint to cover the shiny metal surface.

1. Trace stencil patterns onto frosted side of plastic with marker. Place stencil patterns on protective mat. Using craft knife, cut out each stencil. When cutting out points of crown and jewels, pull knife from tip toward center of each pattern.

2. Referring to photos, position each stencil where desired on surface of cookie sheet. If necessary, secure stencils to surface with tape.

3. Dip dry brush into gold paint. Dab brush onto scrap of paper to remove excess paint. Holding brush perpendicular to cookie sheet surface, lightly pounce brush onto surface to stencil each design. Continue until designs are completely stenciled with thick coat of paint. Carefully lift each stencil. Let dry. Reposition and stencil each design as desired to cover cookie sheet (see photo at left). Let each design dry before repositioning stencil.

4. Referring to photo at left, use dimensional paints to decorate crown and jewel designs. Outline crowns with dots of paint; add details to crowns and jewels with simple dots and lines of paint. Let dry. If desired, spray with acrylic sealer. Let dry.

Index

Contributors

Janet Akhtarshenas
sunflower napkin rings, 82–83

Back Street, Inc., and Jeannie Seward
color-washed watering cans, 60–61

Kay Clark
coppery Christmas ornaments, 106–107

Jane M. Collins
Santa's reindeer, 116–117

Janice Cox
fragrant bath oils, 10–11; tile projects, 92–93

Charlotte Hagood
ribbon rosette pin, 34–35; ribbon-wrapped apples, 102–103

Susan Harrison
appliquéd grapevine shirt, 42–43; coffee-lover's apron, 68–69

Linda Hendrickson
winter wonder pillow, 100–101

Margot Hotchkiss
starry night tree skirt, 98–99; embellished mittens, 104–105

Lori A. Kennedy
pinecone fire starters, 84–85

Heidi Tyline King
trimmed espadrilles, 30–31; naturally festive frames, 108–109

loose ends® and Sarah Stalie
playful pansy lampshade, 70–71

Judith F. Margerum
vintage wreath, 14–15

Connie Matricardi
funny face pins, 76–77; photo-pocket stocking, 110–111

Duffy Morrison
embellished scarves, 36–37; stacked-button sweater, 40–41; ribbon-laced vest, 44–45

Leslie Mueller
victorian preserved bouquet, 22–23

Lelia Gray Neil
painted plates, 90–91; papier-mâché bowls, 94–95; stenciled tray, 140–141

Dondra Parham
foam tray stamp projects, 8–9; wire candle jackets, 20–21; bejeweled barrettes, 38–39; clay pendants, 46–47; decoupage pots, 74–75; sheer sachets, 88–89; Christmas candy cans, 112–113; bookmark critters, 122–123; dimensional photo magnets, 124–125

Catherine Pewitt
veggie baskets, 132–133

Plaid Enterprises, Inc., and Susan Goans Driggers
seashell organizer, 134-135

Plaid Enterprises, Inc., and Sandra McCooey
faux-leather boxes, 80–81

Plaid Enterprises, Inc., Sandra McCooey, and Kindra Werner
magnetic bulletin boards, 18–19

Carol S. Richard
tabletop topiaries, 54–55; fragrant swag, 62–63

Kelley Taylor
plate clock, 26–27; trimmed ornaments, 118–119

Patricia Weaver
handmade paper frames, 12–13; handmade journal, 24–25; charming belt, 48–49; angelic accents projects, 78–79; fabric envelopes, 86–87; holiday door swag, 114–115; moss-covered planters, 136–137

Cyndi Wheeler
baby sleepers, 16–17; appliquéd grapevine shirt, 42–43; pillowcase edgings, 56–57; fabric throw, 66–67; coffee-lover's apron, 68–69; winter wonder pillow, 100–101; painted dish towels, 128–129

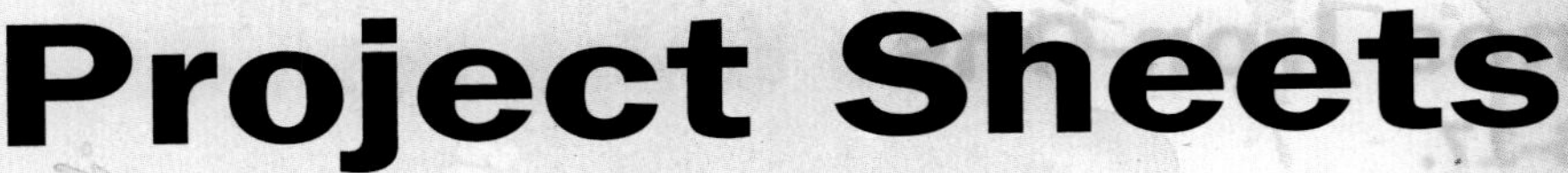

Project Sheets

They're all right here—the designs you need to get started right now on your favorite craft projects.

For iron-on transfers, iron directly from these sheets or photocopy patterns onto iron-on transfer paper and use as instructions indicate.

For stencils, trace patterns onto sheets of frosted template plastic with a black marker. Using a craft knife, cut stencils on shiny side of plastic. Use clear tape to correct any cutting errors.

For cutouts, cut directly from these sheets or copy design on photocopier then cut out.

Note: All patterns are copyright free.

All-in-Ones Iron-Ons

See pages 16–17.

Practice Transfer

Appliquéd Grapevine Shirt Iron-Ons

See pages 42–43.

Practice Transfer

Appliquéd Grapevine Shirt Iron-Ons

See pages 42–43.

Practice Transfer

Grapevine Shirt Iron-Ons

See pages 52–53.

Practice Transfer

Vine Stencil

See pages 52–53.

Coffee-Lover's Apron Iron-On

See pages 68–69.

Practice Transfer

Coffee-Lover's Apron Iron-On

See pages 68–69.

Practice Transfer

Angelic Accents Cutouts

See pages 78–79.

Winter Wonder Iron-Ons

See pages 100–101.

Practice Transfer

Winter Wonder Iron-On

See pages 100–101.

Practice Transfer

Painted Dish Towel Iron-Ons

See pages 128–129.

Painted Dish Towel Iron-Ons

See pages 128–129.

Practice Transfer

Tray Majestic Stencil

See pages 140–141.

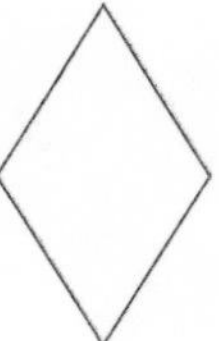

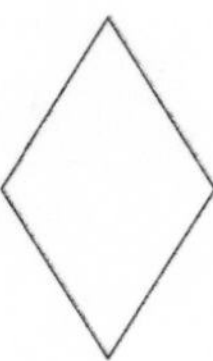